Voyagers

We depend on a network of
people when we explore.

SCHOLASTIC

LITERACY
PLACE®

Copyright acknowledgments and credits appear on page 144, which constitutes an extension of this copyright page.

Copyright © 1996 by Scholastic Inc.   All rights reserved.   Printed in the U.S.A.
                                          ISBN 0-590-49105–9

        3 4 5 6 7 8 9 10   24   02 01 00 99 98 97 96

Take a
Trip to a Travel Agency

We depend on a network of people when we explore.

Travel Data

We rely on many resources when we travel.

SECTION 2

Part of the Crew

A successful journey is the result of a team effort.

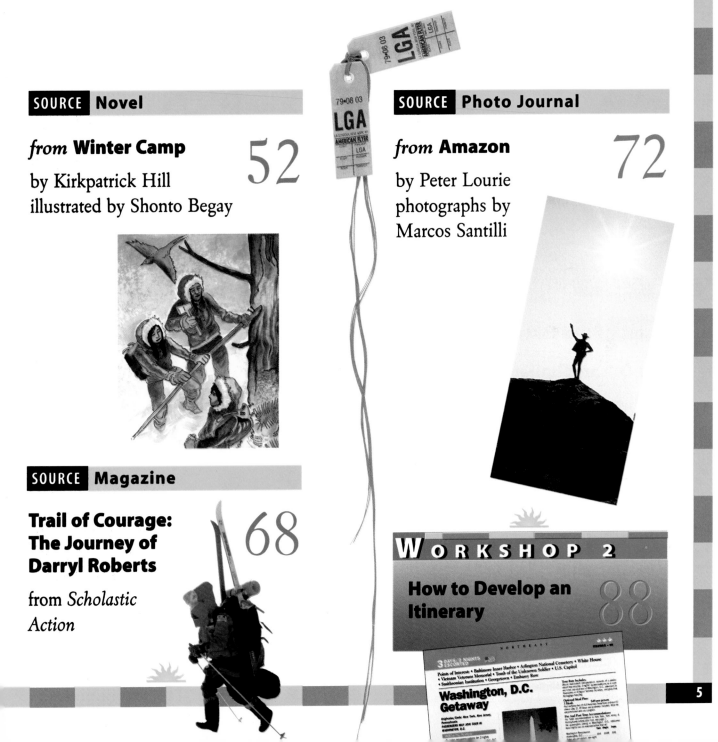

3 DAYS/2 NIGHTS
ESCORTED

Points of Interest: • Baltimore Inner Harbor • Arlington National Cemetery • White House
• Vietnam Veterans Memorial • Tomb of the Unknown Soldier • U.S. Capitol
• Smithsonian Institution • Georgetown • Embassy Row

**Washington, D.C.
Getaway**

Thinking It Through

Teams solve problems when they travel.

Trade Books

The following books accompany this *Voyagers* SourceBook.

Destination: Antarctica

by Robert Swan

AWARD WINNING Author

Flying Free: America's First Black Aviators

by Philip S. Hart

AWARD WINNING Book

The Illyrian Adventure

by Lloyd Alexander

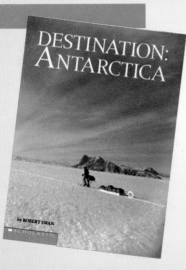

Mr. Popper's Penguins

by Richard and Florence Atwater

Arriving Passengers
🚫 Do Not Enter 🚫

Hotel
Reservations

Ground Transportation
Telephones

West Lobby

We rely on many resources
when we travel.

Travel Data

Read about two
exciting cross-country
airplane trips; one
fictional.

Discover some things
you should know
before you take
your next vacation.

Visit travel agent Marie
French, who relies on
resources from around
the world!

WORKSHOP 1

Create a travel brochure
filled with all kinds of
important facts for travelers.

THE PARTHENON

SOURCE

Coast to Coast

by Betsy Byars

Novel

AWARD
WINNING

Book

from

Coast

Birch's grandfather has always wanted
to fly across the U.S. in his antique
Piper Cub. Much to her surprise, Birch
easily convinces Pop to make the trip on
the spur of the moment. With a map to
guide them, Birch, Pop, and Pop's dog,
Ace, begin the long trip from South
Carolina to California. Along the way,
Birch learns a lot about flying—and
a lot about Pop, too.

to *Coast*

by **Betsy Byars**

illustrated by **Bart Goldman**

"Pop, you know what you forgot to do yesterday?"

It was day five. Pop and Birch had taken off from Las Cruces, New Mexico, at 7:28 and were now flying toward Lordsburg.

"What?"

"You forgot to call out, 'New Mexico!' when we passed El Paso."

"Did I?"

"Yes, you were probably worn out from flying over El Paso. Pop, I don't want to exaggerate, so how long were we over El Paso?"

"Forty-five minutes."

"How high were we?"

"Five hundred feet."

"I believe that because I could actually read the road signs. Next Exit—Las Cruces.

"I actually know every brick and bush in El Paso," she went on, "and there was not one place to land. El Paso has everything in the world but a place to land. The only possibility was, like, the Sun Bowl. Pop, where would we have landed if the engine had quit?"

"Well, it didn't, did it? We made it to Las Cruces."

"But if it had? Would you have landed across the Rio Grande in Mexico? There were some nice fields over there. I always have wanted to visit Mexico."

"Nope."

"Why not?"

"I'd rather crash in the United States."

"Well, I wouldn't. Why?"

"Birch, will you be quiet for five minutes."

"Yes, after I say one thing about Deming. That's Deming up ahead. Deming has more billboards leading into it than any city so far."

Silence.

"You know what my favorite billboards are?"

Silence.

"Those that advertise *The Thing.* Ninety miles to *The Thing.* Don't miss *The Thing.* Pop, what do you think the thing is?"

"I have no idea."

Birch turned around and looked at him. "Pop, I am sitting up here feeling so good and talking my head off and you're going, 'What?...Nope. I have no idea?' So what are you worried about?"

"What makes you think I'm worried?"

"Every time you get stingy with words, I know you're worried."

He worked up a smile. "I'm not worried exactly, but I'm not fond of this head wind."

"Head wind?" Birch looked out the window. "We have a head wind?"

"Actually it's a crosswind."

"That's why all the dust is blowing across the road," she said. She was just beginning to get a feeling for the powerful forces in the air.

Pop said, "Yes."

"It was so calm when we took off. I thought it was going to be a beautiful day. Now there are crosswinds. What happened?"

"The forecast said the winds would be out of the southwest —it's just stronger than they said."

"And I especially wanted to go fast today. I figured out yesterday—you know those big maps they have on the walls at airports? With the neat little string so you can measure how far you've got to go? Well, I measured at Las Cruces and we only have seven hundred more miles. I figured two good days and we'd be there."

"Look down on the ground."

"What am I looking for?" She leaned against the window.

"See the shadow of the plane?"

"Yes, I love shadows from the air. That's how I look for other planes. Like when we're going through a controlled area, the radio will say, 'Three six two, traffic at two o'clock, three miles,' and I look on the ground—for the shadow! Like, look at the telephone poles. The shadows make them look ten times as tall as they are."

"Look at our shadow," he said.

"Oh, I see what you're getting at. Our shadow's at an angle to the road."

"This is what's called crabbing. You've seen a crab going along the beach, haven't you, sort of sideways?"

"Yes."

"That's what we're having to do because of the crosswind."

"You don't like to crab?"

He smiled. "I don't like to land with a crosswind. It's hard to keep the Cub straight on the runway. It wants to ground loop."

"I know what that is—it's like a wheelie."

"I did one ground loop in the service, and the whole landing gear had to be replaced."

"I don't want to waste time replacing things, so let's don't ground loop."

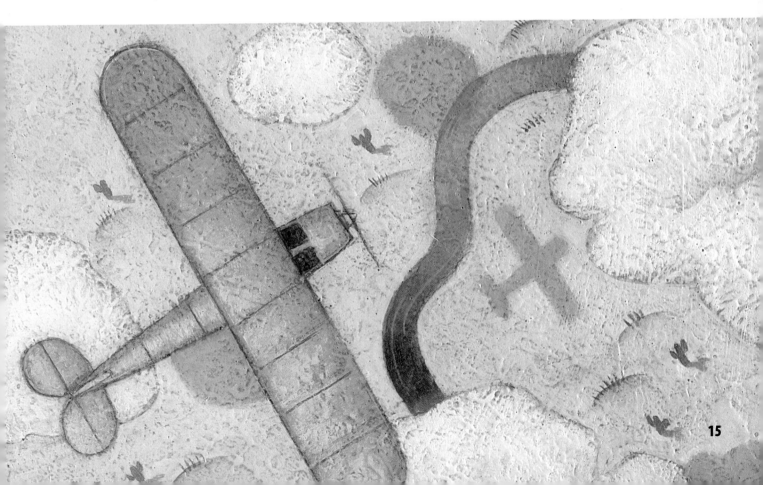

"I'm going to try not to."

Birch looked at her map. "Where are we going to land?"

"The road's turning south now, and we're going to cut straight across and land at Lordsburg. It's an east-west runway, which is bad, but there's a dirt strip into the wind—the Flight Guide calls it Dirt-ruf. Maybe we can land on that."

"I hate to leave the road, don't you?" Birch said. She watched the trucks and cars grow smaller. "It's like leaving civilization."

"We'll be following the pipeline."

"A pipeline is not civilization."

Birch leaned against the window. The land below was sandy, barren except for cactus and sagebrush. Ahead, the sharp peaked hills were blue against the morning sky.

Neither of them spoke.

They crossed a dry creek bed. The plane was so low that Birch could make out animal tracks in the pale sand. "Cow tracks and some little ones," she commented, "jackrabbits or lizards."

"The Continental Divide's along here somewhere," her grandfather said.

"Well, I'm glad there's something along here. Is this a desert?"

"It doesn't qualify."

"Why not? It's desolate enough. Oh, look there's a house—

what do people do way out here in the middle of nowhere?"

"Live."

"Well, that's obvious."

She leaned against the window to look at the gray, weathered house. The cows in the creek bed were so dusty they blended into the ground.

"See the windmill," Pop said. "That tells you something about the wind."

"I would never have noticed that, Pop. You pay attention to things like which way smoke is blowing and what way clothes are blowing on the line and how waves are blowing on lakes. You notice a lot of things, Pop. You're—what's the word I want? Sensitive, I guess, though you're more than that.

"You know, when we started on this trip, there was something I wanted you to tell me, and I couldn't ask. I wasn't ready. And then when I talked to my dad on the phone, he said he'd talk to me when I got home. Which relieved me.

"And then I realized, Pop, that I was relieved partly because I wanted to hear it from you—whatever it was. Because I am probably closer to you than I am to anybody else in the world. And if you told me, I would take it better. I mean that as a compliment."

Pop said, "What are you muttering about up there?"

"Oh, nothing. I was paying you a compliment."

"I'd like to hear it when we get down from here."

Birch nodded. "I'd like to tell you—when we get down from here." She and Pop fell silent then.

They passed another creek bed, and Birch checked the tracks. "More jackrabbits, cows, I swear I see horned toad prints."

The foothills were seamed with dry washes now. Stunted shrubs had collected in the deep wrinkles.

"Well, do you feel better?" Pop said. "We're meeting back up with the interstate."

"I'd forgotten about that." She looked up at the line of traffic in the distance, no bigger now than a string of beads. "Yes, I do feel better. I like company."

"And that's Lordsburg ahead. I'm going to call them on the radio and see if it's safe to land on the dirt."

"Well, even I know it's windy when the wind sock is sticking out like a pole," Birch said.

"Be quiet," Pop said.

He turned on his radio and set the frequency. "Lordsburg Unicom, Piper Cub three oh three six two."

"Plus, we are the only fools in the air. I have not seen one other plane."

Pop waited. When there was no answer, he said again, "Lordsburg Unicom, how do you hear Piper Cub three oh three six two?"

"They've probably closed up and gone home," Birch muttered to herself.

A voice from the radio said, "Cub three six two, Lordsburg. Hear you five square now. Go ahead."

"Lordsburg, Cub three six two is ten miles east, over the interstate, landing Lordsburg. Say wind and traffic and what is the condition of runway one-nine?"

"Cub three six two, wind is two zero zero at about twenty knots, gusting to twenty-five or thirty, favoring runway one-nine. No reported traffic. Runway one-nine is dirt but condition is good. No problem for a Cub. Over."

"Roger, Lordsburg. We'll be coming up on left base for one nine in a couple of minutes. Keep me posted if there is any significant wind change."

"Rog, three six two."

"It looks all right," her grandfather said.

"How fast is twenty knots?"

"Don't talk to me now."

"Well, it's my life too!"

"Between twenty-five and thirty miles an hour!"

They approached the airport in silence. Pop turned the J-3 on final. He said into the radio, "Lordsburg traffic, Cub three six two turning final for one nine."

Birch could see the runway below—dirt with yellow arrows on the edge made out of automobile tires.

"Belt tight?" he asked.

"You bet."

Now that they were heading directly into the wind, the J-3 hardly seemed to be moving over the ground at all. As the plane began to sink toward the runway, the turbulent air coming over the hills to the west began to bounce the plane around.

Birch reached for the support bars and held on tight. Behind her Ace barked in sharp protest.

The J-3 touched down on the hard earth once, twice, and finally a third time. Then it slowed to a stop at the intersection to the ramp.

"Now the fun begins," Pop said tensely.

"What? We're down!"

"We've got to turn one hundred ten degrees to the ramp. It's one thing when the wind is blowing straight toward us, but when we turn and that wind gets under the wing—Birch, you better get out and hold it."

"What? The airplane?"

"Hold onto the wingtip and steady it."

"Pop, I weigh one hundred pounds. I couldn't hold an airplane down, especially if the wind wanted to take it up."

She undid her seat belt and climbed out. "Now I have done everything," she mumbled. She went carefully around the back of the airplane, as Pop had taught her, and took the left wingtip.

As the plane started around the corner, the wind gusted and tried to lift it. Birch opened her mouth to scream as the wing picked her up on her toes.

"I've got it," a voice said in her ear.

Birch whipped her hair from her eyes and turned. A boy was behind her. His hand stretched around hers onto the wingtip. It was a miracle. Even if it had been an ugly boy, it would have been a miracle, but this boy was not ugly.

Birch was aware she could let go, but she didn't. Together the two of them walked the J-3 around the corner, guiding it to the ramp.

Pop cut the engine and said, "Let's get this thing tied down before the wind blows it over."

A man with a sun-cured face came out to help them, but the boy already had the left wing tied down. His movements had a western quickness, like something out of a rodeo, Birch thought.

"It's too much wind for me," Pop told the man.

"For me too," Birch told the boy. "I bet we were the only people in the air today."

"The only ones we've seen."

The boy moved to the right wing. Birch moved with him. "Even our dog—this is Ace—" Birch reached into the cockpit.

"Hello, Ace." The boy paused to scratch him behind one ear.

"It was even too much for Ace. He barked for the first time since we left South Carolina."

The boy finished the right wing and moved to the tail of the plane. Birch went along.

"You folks are from South Carolina?" he asked.

"Yes, where are *you* from?"

"Here."

"Oh."

"You folks planning to spend the night in Lordsburg?" the man asked.

Birch said quickly, "I am. I promised myself that if I got down safely, I wasn't going to get back in the airplane today." She looked at Pop.

He said, "I pretty much promised myself the same thing." He took off his glasses and blotted his face on his sleeve.

"My son'll be glad to drive you to a motel."

"We'd appreciate it." Pop looked at his watch. "Birch, it's only nine o'clock in the morning. What are we going to do all day?"

Birch glanced at the boy. The dry hot wind seemed to be blowing them together. "Oh, I don't know. . . recover."

The man said, "Pete, get the car and drive these folks into town."

"I'll be right back."

Pop checked the ropes again, and Birch said, "Pop, that boy—Pete—tied them perfectly. He—"

Pop looked up. "Where'd Ace get to? Ace!"

A mouse-colored dog with a flea collar was disappearing around the hangar. Ace was trotting behind, trying to get the dog's attention.

"That'll do, Ace," Pop said.

Birch ran after Ace and scooped him up. "That dog's too big for you. You're not in her league." She brought Ace back to the J-3.

In the parking lot, the boy was starting an old station wagon.

"Pop," she said, "you know what worries me when we have a day like today—or yesterday?" She grinned. "Or the day before that?"

"What?"

"That we're going to have to turn around and go home. We're going to do it all over again, only the other way. Like, we'll hang over El Paso for forty-five minutes again, we'll go over those Van Horn mountains, we'll land on that access road, we'll—"

"The reason we're flying so low is because of the head winds. The higher we get, the stronger the winds are. On the way home, we'll have tail winds. We'll be at five thousand feet instead of five hundred. You won't even recognize it as the same place."

"Is that a promise?" She broke off as the station wagon stopped beside them. "I'll ride in the front with Pete," Birch said quickly. "You and Ace just sit in the back and relax."

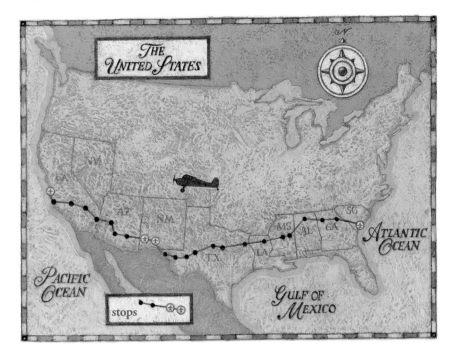

from

The Meadville Tribune

TUESDAY, SEPTEMBER 21, 1993

Country Rolls Out Tarmac For Girl Pilot

Vicki Van Meter and her instructor depart from Augusta, Maine, to begin their cross-country journey.

FROM TRIBUNE AND WIRE REPORTS

NEW CUMBERLAND, PA— A sixth-grader landed a small plane outside Harrisburg Monday on her way across the country and possibly into the record books.

Victoria Van Meter, 11, of Meadville, touched down at Capital City Airport at about 12:20 P.M., accompanied by her flight instructor Bob Baumgartner.

The two left Augusta, Maine, Monday morning and hope to end their 2,900 mile journey to San Diego on Thursday.

Van Meter said she had a little trouble finding the airport, but otherwise the flight was trouble-free.

If successful, she will become the youngest female pilot to fly cross-country,

Corinne Van Meter offers her daughter some last-minute encouragement.

the youngest to fly 2,900 miles and the youngest to complete an east-to-west cross-country flight.

East-west flights are more challenging because pilots often are forced to fly against the wind, Baumgartner said.

The government has no age restriction for pilots who fly with an instructor, according to Blain Hackett, spokesman for the Federal Aviation Administration.

Van Meter does all the flying, navigating and communication while in the air, Baumgartner said. He said her performance so far was excellent.

Her godmother, Alice Moberg of Latrobe, was at the airport to meet her.

Moberg said she doesn't worry about Vicki's safety when she flies.

"There really isn't any worry. They know what they're doing," she said.

Moberg said Van Meter has been flying for almost a year and has always had an adventurous spirit.

"She has not been confined to the things that little girls normally do," Moberg said.

The young pilot said she'd like to become an astronaut. But if she doesn't, she'd like to

continue flying planes.

"If I can't work for NASA, I hope to work for a commercial airline as a pilot," said the young aviator, standing aside the single-engine Cessna 172 she pilots.

In honor of her arrival, Harrisburg declared Sept. 20 Vicki Van Meter Day.

Sen. Robert Robbins, R-Mercer, met Vicki at the airport to present her with a citation of congratulation and to take her to lunch.

Her parents were among about a dozen well-wishers who huddled in the 30-degree weather to watch her take off.

Peter Thompson, president of the Kennebec Valley Chamber of Commerce, presented Van Meter with a bottle of water from the Atlantic Ocean to take on her journey and lent her his jacket as she waited to be interviewed by Bryant Gumbel on NBC-TV's *Today* program via a satellite hookup.

In honor of Van Meter's departure, the mayor of Augusta declared today Victoria Van Meter Day, Thompson said.

"This is something she'll never, ever be able to forget," said the girl's mother,

Vicki's cross-country journey has earned her many honors, including an invitation to sit in a NASA T-38 astronaut trainer.

Corinne, who, with her husband James, was taking commercial flights to join their daughter at each of her overnight stops.

"We're really proud of our little girl," added her father, who said he held a pilot's license himself 30 years ago but no longer flies.

Her itinerary for today is: leave Columbus at 7 A.M.;

Vicki Van Meter and Bob Baumgartner consult Vicki's flight log.

land at St. Louis, 11:15 A.M.; leave St. Louis, 12:30 P.M.; and arrive at Wiley Post Airport in Oklahoma City, 5:45 P.M.

Following her journey, Vicki is welcomed home with a rally at her local airport.

Wednesday's schedule: leave Oklahoma City, 7 A.M.; arrive at Albuquerque, NM, 11:45 A.M.; leave Albuquerque, 12:30 P.M.; and arrive at Phoenix, AZ, 3:40 P.M.

Thursday she will leave Phoenix at 11 A.M. and is scheduled to arrive in San Diego at 1:00 P.M. Thursday.

Thompson, in a phone call to *The Meadville Tribune*, said Vicki had toured many historical sites in Augusta Sunday and had been interviewed by three television networks.

"It was a fun time," he said.

City girl is high-flying pilot

By JEAN SHANLEY

While Vicki's excited about the flight, the 11-year-old has more to do than just going to the airport and hopping into a plane. She must call for weather reports, check the flight plan, and plan accordingly, taking into account any inclement weather she might be facing.

All information must be used to determine a flight plan. Vicki reviews all the technical information that she must check. Sounding like a veteran pilot, she explains what it all means and what changes are made because of weather and other factors.

She also must do what is known as a preflight inspection of the plane—walking around the craft to be sure everything is okay, including making sure no bird has built a nest in the engine and that the propeller has no nicks. She has a checklist that must be completed before she leaves, she said. She is proud she has gotten very good at doing the preflight inspection.

Flight log in hand, Vicki exits her plane at the Columbus, Ohio, airport.

NBC • TODAY SHOW

transcript of interview Vicki Van Meter/Bryant Gumbel
September 20, 1993 • 7:00–9:00 A.M.

BRYANT GUMBEL: At a time when most girls her age are getting adjusted to a new school year, 11-year-old Vicki Van Meter is out to break some records. Just a short while ago she took off from the airport at Augusta, Maine, on an historic transcontinental flight to San Diego, California. When she arrives there on Thursday, she'll become the youngest female pilot to fly cross country, the youngest person to fly 2,900 miles, and the youngest person to complete an east to west transcontinental cross-country flight. All that, and she only started taking flying lessons last fall. Shortly before takeoff, I talked with Vicki and her flight instructor, Bob Baumgartner, who'll be accompanying her on the trip. And I asked Vicki to explain her great desire to fly.

MS. VICKI VAN METER: Well, I hopefully want to work for NASA some day, so I just decided to fly.

MR. GUMBEL: I understand you just started taking lessons a year ago. Has learning to fly come difficult for you, or has it been pretty easy? What do you think?

MS. VAN METER: Well, it's sort of in-between. I had to go to ground school. It's a special pilot school, and it was hard doing that and my regular school work at the same time. So parts of it were hard.

MR. GUMBEL: Let's talk about this transcontinental flight that you're starting on today. Why are you doing this?

MS. VAN METER: Well, because it's something challenging that I can do, and it's going to be setting three world records. So it's pretty neat.

MR. GUMBEL: What's going to be the toughest part of the trip for you?

MS. VAN METER: Probably staying awake and getting up early in the morning, but also talking on the radios, because it's hard listening to someone, and there's static and stuff.

MR. GUMBEL: Tell me a little bit about your flight plan. What does it look like, and what kind of weather are you heading into?

MS. VAN METER: Well, today I'm going to be going down to Harrisburg, and then from there to Columbus. And from here to Harrisburg it looks pretty good, but from Harrisburg to Columbus it looks a little shaky. There won't be good weather.

MR. GUMBEL: Let me talk to Bob for just a little bit. How difficult is this task that you and Vicki are—are setting off on?

MR. BOB BAUMGARTNER: Well, it's a pretty difficult journey. We're going to see all kinds of terrain on our way across the country. We have the mountains here in the Northeast, and then we've got the Rockies and Coastal Range toward the end of the flight, plus we're crossing the Plains States. So we're going to see it all on this trip.

MR. GUMBEL: How much will she really be flying the plane, and how much will you be doing?

MR. BAUMGARTNER: She'll be doing all the flying, all the navigating, and most, if not all of the communicating.

MR. GUMBEL: One final question, Vicki, aren't you supposed to be in school this week?

MS. VAN METER: Yeah, my teachers are excusing me from school these two weeks, but when I come back they're going to help me, and I'm going to be doing the work after school and catching up.

MR. GUMBEL: I suspect you're getting a pretty good education this week anyway.

MS. VAN METER: Yeah.

MR. GUMBEL: Hey, Vicki, Bob, good luck to both of you. Thank you.

MS. VAN METER: OK, thanks.

MR. BAUMGARTNER: Thank you, Bryant.

MR. GUMBEL: Vicki's promised us a return date later in the week after she makes it to San Diego. We'll talk with her then. This is *Today* on NBC.

Vicki chats with *Today Show* host Bryant Gumbel.

from Going Places

Planning Your Trip

Getting ready for a trip can be almost as much fun as taking one. The first step is to gather information, so you'll know as much as possible about the area you're going to visit. Once your research is completed, it's time to make an itinerary, a detailed plan describing where you'll go and how you'll get there, where you'll stay, and what you hope to see and do.

In preparing for your trip, you might also want to think about how you'll remember it when it's over. One easy way to preserve your memories is to write yourself a picture postcard each day of the trip, and mail it to yourself. When you get home you'll have an illustrated journal of your experiences waiting for you right there in your mailbox.

Gathering Information

The more you know about your destination, the more you'll be able to enjoy your trip. That's because planning ahead allows you to discover the possibilities that are awaiting you. You can plan your time to make sure you don't miss the places and activities at the top of your list. It isn't much fun to travel to a distant city and discover that the museum you wanted to visit is closed on Mondays or that the baseball game you hoped to see is sold out. Planning ahead can help you avoid disappointments like these. It can also open your eyes to activities and attractions you may not even have heard of when your family decided where to go.

by Harriet Webster
illustrated by Santiago Cohen

To begin your research, head for your local library. Your librarian can help you find the names and addresses of local, state, and regional tourist bureaus and chambers of commerce that serve the areas you plan to visit. Write to them well in advance of your trip, requesting brochures, maps, calendars of events, and any other information you need (how to get tickets to that ball game, for example). It is their business to promote tourism, so they will be happy to help you.

Once you have collected and studied the material, you can sit down with your parents and plan what you would like to do each day of the trip. If you are traveling by car, you may want to plan brief side trips to places of interest along the way.

Your librarian can also help you find books to read that will help you learn about the history of the place you are going to visit and about people who lived there. The librarian may also know about works of fiction that are set in the area you plan to visit.

············· *Packing Your Backpack* ·············

Whether your travels will last a day or a month, you will want to take along a small backpack containing supplies that will make the trip more enjoyable. The items you pack will depend upon your interests and where you are going. If you are traveling a long distance, a small radio or tape recorder equipped with a headset can help you pass the time. A deck of cards is also useful, and so is a good book, especially if the story relates to your destination.

To keep a record of your trip, take along a notebook and several pens or pencils. Write the date at the top of the page, and perhaps a note describing the weather. Then use the notebook as a journal, recording any thoughts or impressions you wish to store away. Some people like to write in their journals at the same time each day, perhaps before going to sleep at night. Others prefer to scribble notes throughout the day, whenever the mood strikes. Either way works well. If you want to write postcards to friends, enter their addresses in the back of your journal before you leave so they will be handy when you need them.

If you like to draw, you may prefer to record your impressions in pictures; pack a sketchpad and some markers or other simple art supplies.

Traveling by car? Include a road map so that you will be able to keep track of your progress. If you are traveling by plane, add to your pack the free air-route map you will find in the seat pocket. Other handy items to include are small plastic bags (for collecting), white glue, and string, all of which come in useful at unexpected times. Consider bringing a small flashlight and a magnifying glass. If you plan to take photos, pack your camera and film in your backpack so that they're always nearby when you need them.

In supplying your backpack, the main idea is to stick to items that you want to have easily available throughout the day. But if you stuff it too full, you'll have trouble finding what you need. With a little practice, you will figure out what is right for you.

Money Around the World

One challenge when traveling in a foreign country is getting used to using a different system of money. Before traveling abroad, you'll need to know what kind of currency is used, and the amount of the currency you'll get in exchange for each U.S. dollar.

Country	Name of Currency
Australia	Australian dollar
Great Britain	pound
Canada	Canadian dollar
France	franc
Germany	mark
Greece	drachma
Hong Kong	Hong Kong dollar
Israel	shekel
Japan	yen
Kenya	shilling
Mexico	peso
South Korea	won
Uganda	Ugandan dollar

Five Ways to Keep Busy While Standing in Line

TIME TRAVEL

Did you know that when kids are getting up for school in Cleveland, Ohio, at 7 o'clock in the morning, it's 10 o'clock at night in Sydney, Australia? Chances are that when you travel far from home, you'll end up in a different time zone.

Standing in line is a sometimes annoying, often necessary part of taking trips. Important monuments, tourist attractions, and exciting rides just naturally draw crowds, as do popular restaurants and movies. Here are some ways to keep your mind busy while you wait for your turn.

1. Make up stories about the people around you.

2. Determine the mood of the people in line. What do their expressions tell you about what they are feeling? Study their body language. Is the kid ahead of you kicking up dirt with his heel because he's bored or angry at his parents for making him come along? What do people do with their hands when they're excited? When they're frustrated?

3. Eavesdrop. Listen to what the people around you are saying. What do other people talk about while they wait in line? Why do people discuss the weather so much?

4. Take a survey. How many people in the line are wearing sunglasses? How many children under the age of six are in the line? How many people over the age of seventy? How does this compare to the line you stood in yesterday?

5. Bone up on the place you are about to visit by reading brochures and guidebooks. Then you'll know just what to look for.

Documenting Your Travels
with Photographs

Lots of people love to snap pictures as they travel. They take photos of the famous places they visit, of family members and people they meet along the way, of pretty views. The pictures get developed, admired, and shoved into the back of a drawer. The problem comes when you pull them out a few years later, and you may have forgotten where they were taken or who the strangers are. If you like to take lots of pictures (and taking lots is one of the best ways of getting some really good ones), promise yourself that you'll take the time to sit down and label your pictures and mount them in an album as a permanent record of your experience.

For a complete record of your trip, you might consider expanding your photo album into a scrapbook by combining your pictures with other bits of memorabilia you have collected on the trip: ticket stubs, clippings from a local newspaper, menus, brochures, pressed flowers, postcards, theater programs, and the like. To make it even more complete, use index cards to write out your memories about the places and people you visited and the things you did. Then add these to your album.

Another way to use photographs to document your trip is to specialize. If you visit a large city, for example, you might decide to concentrate on photographs of skyscrapers.

If you visit a national park, you might choose to take pictures of all the types of trees you see. You might decide to photograph only people: the man who pumps gas, the farmer on the tractor, the elderly man feeding pigeons in the park, the policeman controlling the traffic. Whatever your subject, try to get shots from a distance as well as close-ups. Snap your subject at different times of day, from different angles.

Still another way to approach photography is to take pictures with the purpose of using them to tell a story. You might photograph the view from your hotel window at intervals throughout the day, showing how the mountains look at dawn, at midmorning, at noon, in the late afternoon, at sunset, and at dusk. Or take pictures of the woods before, during, and after a snowstorm. If you are spending a week at the seashore, shoot the same strip of shoreline at the same hour each day, reflecting the way in which shifting tides affect the contours of the beach. If you are going on a fishing expedition, take photos of your family carrying the necessary gear, baiting hooks, casting the line, pulling in the fish, gutting it, cooking it, and eating it.

After you have had your pictures developed, label, arrange, and mount them. What do they tell you about the place you have visited? Do your photos bring back memories of sounds, smells, or tastes? Postcards usually provide an excellent record of major sites and scenes. What is special about *your* photographs is that they represent what caught *your* eye. They are a record of your unique point of view and they represent your personal experience.

COAST-TO-COAST
AMTRAK'S SUNSET LIMITED
LOS ANGELES TO MIAMI

Los Angeles…Phoenix…San Antonio… New Orleans…Jacksonville…Miami

2			◄ Train Number ► [a]		1
Dp. LAX SuTuFr [d] [b]			◄ Days of Operation ► [f] [c]		Ar. LAX WeFrMo
ReadDown	Mile	▼	[e]	Symbol	▲ Read Up
			(Southern Pacific Lines)		
10 50P	0	Dp	Los Angeles, CA ✳ 🚌 [g] (PT)	📷 ♿	Ar 7 00A
11 34P	34		Pomona, CA	● ♿	5 26A
57	39		Ontario, CA	●	57
1 25A	130		Indio, CA (Palm Springs) (PT)	● ♿	3 29A
69 4 12A	253		Yuma, AZ (MST)	●	69 2 38A
69 8 25A	426		Phoenix, AZ ✳	📷 ♿	69 11 30P
69 8 47A	434		Tempe, AZ	● ♿	69 9 51P
69 9 47A	480		Coolidge, AZ	● ♿	69 8 44P
69 10 47A	545		Tucson, AZ ✳	📷 ♿	69 7 40P
69 12 03P	592		Benson, AZ (MST)	● ♿	69 6 38P
2 00P	708		Lordsburg, NM (MT)	● ♿	4 42P
2 51P	767		Deming, NM (MT)	● ♿	3 52P
5 05P 5 25P	855	Ar Dp	El Paso, TX ✳ (MT) (Ciudad Juarez, Mex.)	📷 ♿	Dp 2 25P Ar 2 05P
9 59P	1073		Alpine, TX (Big Bend Nat'l Park) (CT)	● ♿	11 10A
11 40P	1165		Sanderson, TX	● ♿	9 06A
2 07A	1291		Del Rio, TX	● ♿	6 37A
5 50A 6 35A	1460	Ar Dp	San Antonio, TX ✳	📷 ♿	Dp 3 35A Ar 3 05A
11 15A	1670		Houston, TX (Galveston, Dallas 🚌) ✳	📷 ♿	10 30P
1 03P	1752		Beaumont, TX (Port Arthur)	● ♿	7 49P
2 30P	1814		Lake Charles, LA	● ♿	6 32P
3 48P	1888		Lafayette, LA (Baton Rouge 🚌)	● ♿	5 15P
4 10P	1906		New Iberia, LA	● ♿	4 50P
5 29P	1977		Schriever, LA (Houma/Thibodaux)	● ♿	3 31P
7 50P	2033	Ar	New Orleans, LA ✳ (CT)	📷 ♿	Dp 2 15P
Dp. NOL TuThSu					Dp. NOL MoWeSa
			(CSX)		
11 00A	2033	Dp	New Orleans, LA ✳ (CT)	📷 ♿	Ar 11 55A
12 07A	2089		Bay St. Louis, MS	● ♿	10 05A
12 25A	2104		Gulfport, MS	● ♿	9 42A
12 40A	2117		Biloxi, MS	● ♿	9 25A
1 10A	2137		Pascagoula, MS	● ♿	9 00A
2 00A	2177		Mobile, AL ✳	📷 ♿	8 25A
2 48A	2222		Atmore, AL	● ♿	7 25A
4 35A 4 50A	2281	Ar Dp	Pensacola, FL ✳	📷 ♿	Dp 5 55A Ar 5 40A
5 50A	2331		Crestview, FL (Ft. Walton Beach)	● ♿	4 00A
7 10A	2397		Chipley, FL (Panama City) (CT)	● ♿	2 38A
10 20A	2485		Tallahassee, FL ✳ (ET)	📷 ♿	1 45A
11 40A	2540		Madison, FL	● ♿	12 11A
12 33P	2590		Lake City, FL (Gainesville)	● ♿	11 11P
2 30P	2652	Ar	Jacksonville, FL ✳	📷 ♿	Dp 10 10P
Dp. JAX WeFrMo					Dp. JAX SuTuFr
2 45P	2652	Dp	Jacksonville, FL ✳	📷 ♿	Ar 9 55P
3 48P	2711		Palatka, FL	● ♿	8 10P
4 33P	2763		DeLand, FL (Daytona Beach) ✳	🏫 ♿	7 24P
4 55P	2779		Sanford, FL	📷 ♿	7 05P
5 20P	2798		Winter Park, FL	📷 ♿	6 42P
5 50P	2803		Orlando, FL (WALT DISNEY WORLD®) ✳	📷 ♿	6 28P
6 07P	2821		Kissimmee, FL (WALT DISNEY WORLD®)	📷	6 00P
Amtrak Thruway Bus Connection—Winter Haven, FL/Tampa, FL/St. Petersburg, FL—Schedules Follow					
7 02P	2859		Winter Haven, FL (Tampa–St. Petersburg)	📷 ♿	5 12P
7 40P	2900		Sebring, FL	📷 ♿	4 33P
8 15P	2942		Okeechobee, FL	● ♿	3 58P
9 15P	3003		West Palm Beach, FL	📷 ♿	3 05P
9 35P	3021		Delray Beach, FL	○ ♿	2 30P
9 50P	3032		Deerfield Beach, FL (Boca Raton)	📷 ♿	2 17P
10 08P	3046		Ft. Lauderdale, FL (Pt. Everglades) ✳	📷 ♿	2 00P
10 20P	3053		Hollywood, FL	📷 ♿	1 49P
11 10P	3066	Ar	Miami, FL (Key West) ✳ (ET)	📷 ♿	Dp 1 30P
Ar. MIA WeFrMo					Dp. MIA SuTuFr

HOW TO READ AN AMTRAK TRAIN SCHEDULE

Amtrak's Sunset Limited train runs coast to coast between Los Angeles, California, and Miami, Florida, making many stops along the way. This timetable allows Amtrak to tell its customers lots of information about the train in very little space.

[a] Train number indicates what the train will be called as it journeys across the country. From Miami to L.A., it's called #1, and from L.A. to Miami, it's #2.

[b] This column shows times of arrival and departure at every stop from L.A. to Miami.

[c] This column shows arrival and departure times at every stop from Miami to L.A. Read this column from the bottom up.

[d] This column shows cumulative mileage as the train crosses the country. It will travel a total of 3,066 miles each way.

[e] This column lists the towns and cities where the train makes its stops.

[f] The symbols in this column tell whether services such as wheelchair accessibility and express shipping are available at each stop.

[g] Symbols next to the name of the city indicate special services available through that station, such as connecting buses and vacation packages.

YOUR TICKET TO TRAVEL

If you travel to a foreign country, you'll need more than a suitcase. World travelers almost always carry a passport, which is an official document that identifies who they are and what country they live in. The U.S. government issues passports to all citizens. If you need a passport, your local post office can tell you how and where to get one.

What Does "Old" Really Mean?

Here's a quick experiment to try. Write the word "old" across the top of a piece of paper. Now jot down any thoughts, things, places, ideas, or people the word brings to mind.

Now think about the words you've written. Sometimes "old" means useless, broken, or out of style. At other times, it implies wisdom, great value (as in a very old baseball card), or fragility. Do the words on your list fall into these categories?

"Old" can also mean steeped in history, and that's the way it is used when applied to many places that attract tourists. You visit the natural history museum to see the exhibit of dinosaur fossils. They're certainly old. Perhaps you will visit homes where famous people were born and lived. You might visit a battle-field, a one-room schoolhouse, a fort, a clipper ship, a re-created village. All of them are called "old," but what does that really mean? After all,

Abraham Lincoln's stovepipe hat is certainly old, but it's nowhere near as old as George Washington's false teeth. Old is a comparative term. It implies that something is older than something else. An old house in Utah might be a couple of hundred years younger than an old house in New England, but that's because Utah was settled much later than New England.

One way to keep a clear picture of how long ago one event occurred compared to another is to draw a time line depicting the events, places, and artifacts you encounter on your trip. Use a roll of paper about six feet long, or staple together lengthwise six (or more) pieces of blank paper. Figure out the earliest period in time represented on your trip (for example, the date the Pilgrims landed at Plymouth Rock) and the most recent (*Old Ironsides* launched). Make a broad horizontal line across the center of your long

strip of paper. Write 1620 at the far left edge and then write 1797 at the far right edge, noting the significance of each date. Write 1625, 1650, 1675, 1700, 1725, 1750, and 1775 (or any guide numbers you choose) along the line at even intervals. Now you have a time line representing the period of history covered on your trip.

Each time you visit a place, be it the *Mayflower II,* the recreated Plymouth Plantation, *Old Ironsides,* Paul Revere's house, the Old North Church, the Bunker Hill Monument, or the Boston Tea Party Museum,

enter a brief description of the site and its significance at the appropriate place on your time line. You might also decide to glue on postcards or other mementoes, or to illustrate the time line with your own drawings. Roll it up and fasten it with paper clips whenever you finish working on it. When you get home, you will have a historical record of your travels ready to mount on your wall as a mural. Best of all, you'll have a visual reminder that keys you in on how different moments in history relate to each other. Sometimes old is just not new, and sometimes it is ancient!

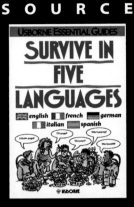

Usborne Essential Guides

SURVIVE IN FIVE LANGUAGES

☒ english ☐ french ☐ german
☐ italian ☐ spanish

Language
Phrase Book

from

SURVIVE IN FIVE LANGUAGES

by Ceris Farnes

HI CIAO

You can't learn a foreign language overnight, but if you visit another country, you'll need to know at least a few key words and phrases. That's where a language phrase book comes in handy. See if you can pronounce the words and phrases given here in five different languages.

ABSOLUTE ESSENTIALS

French	Spanish	Italian	German

USEFUL PHRASES

Do you speak English?

French	Spanish	Italian	German
Vous parlez anglais?[1] *Voo par-leh o(n)-gleh?*	**¿Habla inglés?**[1] *¿A-bla een-glehs?*	**Parla inglese?**[1] *´Par-la eeng-´leh-zeh?*	**Sprechen Sie Englisch?**[1] *Shprekhen zee english?*
Tu parles anglais?[2] *Tew parl o(n)-gleh?*	**¿Hablas inglés?**[2] *¿A-blas een-glehs?*	**Parli inglese?**[2] *´Par-lee eeng-´leh-zeh?*	**Sprichst du Englisch?**[2] *Shprikhst doo english?*

I don't understand.

French	Spanish	Italian	German
Je ne comprends pas. *Je(r) ne(r) ko(m)-pro(n) pa.*	**No entiendo.** *Noh ehn-tyehn-doh.*	**Non capisco.** *Non ca-pee-scoh.*	**Ich verstehe das nicht.** *Ikh fer-shtaye(r) dass nikht.*

Can you say that again?

French	Spanish	Italian	German
Vous pouvez répéter ça?[1] *Voo poo-veh reh-peh-teh sa?*	**¿Puede repetir?**[1] *¿Pweh-deh reh-peh-teer?*	**Può ripetere?**[1] *Pwoh ree-´peh-teh-reh?*	**Können Sie das noch einmal sagen?**[1] *Ku(r)nen zee dass nokh eyn-mal zahgen?*
Tu peux répéter ça?[2] *Tew pe(r) reh-peh-teh sa?*	**¿Puedes repetir?**[2] *¿Pweh-dehs reh-peh-teer?*	**Puoi ripetere?**[2] *Pwoy ree-´peh-teh-reh?*	**Kannst du das noch einmal sagen?**[2] *Kanst doo dass nokh eyn-mal zahgen?*

English	French	Spanish	Italian	German

English	French	Spanish	Italian	German
hello	**bonjour** *bo(n)-joor*	**hola** *oh-la*	**salve** *´sal-veh*	**hallo** *ha-llo*
goodbye	**au revoir** *o re(r)-vwa(r)*	**adiós** *a-dyohs*	**arrivederci** *ar-ree-veh-´dehr-chee*	**auf Wiedersehen** *owf veeder-zayen*
hi	**salut** *sa-lew*	**hola** *oh-la*	**ciao** *chow*	**hi, hallo** *hi, hallo*
bye	**salut** *sa-lew*	**adiós** *a-dyohs*	**ciao** *chow*	**tschüs** *shewss*
good morning	**bonjour** *bo(n)-joor*	**buenos días** *bweh-nohs dee-as*	**buon giorno** *bwon ´jor-noh*	**guten Morgen** *goo-ten morgen*
good night	**bonne nuit** *bon-nwee*	**buenas noches** *bweh-nas noh-tchehs*	**buona notte** *bwoh-na ´not-teh*	**gute Nacht** *goo-te(r) nahkht*
Mr., Sir	**Monsieur** *me(r)-sye(r)*	**Señor** *seh-nyohr*	**Signor/Signore** *see-´nyòhr/see-´nyoh-reh*	**Herr** *hair*
Mrs., Madam	**Madame** *ma-dahm*	**Señora** *seh-nyoh-ra*	**Signora** *see-´nyoh-ra*	**Frau** *frow*
Miss	**Mademoiselle** *mad-mwa-zell*	**Señorita** *seh-nyoh-ree-ta*	**Signorina** *see-nyoh-´ree-na*	**Fräulein** *fro(r)-line*
yes	**oui** *oo-ee*	**sí** *see*	**sì** *see*	**ja** *yah*
no	**non** *no(n)*	**no** *noh*	**no** *noh*	**nein** *nine*
please	**s'il vous plaît,[1]** **s'il te plaît[2]** *seel-voo-pleh,* *seel-te(r)-pleh*	**por favor** *pohr fa-bohr*	**per favore** *pehr fa-´voh-reh*	**bitte** *bitte(r)*
thank you	**merci** *mair-see*	**gracias** *gra-thyas*	**grazie** *´gra-tsyeh*	**danke** *danke(r)*

Marie French

Travel Agent

Marie French and **her team** *work hard* to **make traveling** easy.

Too busy to plan a trip? Looking for the best prices on transportation? Perhaps you simply prefer to leave the planning to an expert? Travel agents employ a network of contacts, in places near and far, to make sure your voyage is worry free. Read on to find out how Marie French and her fellow agents work together to ensure smooth sailing for their clients.

PROFILE

Name: Marie French

Occupation: travel agent

Education: Harper College

Interests: interior design, photography

Favorite travel destination: Rome and Israel for history, Greek islands for relaxation

Favorite travel magazine: *Travel Weekly*

Favorite travel movie: *Raiders of the Lost Ark*

Souvenir collection: polished stones from all over the world

QUESTIONS
for Marie French

Find out how *Marie French* and her *colleagues* make plans for people *on the go*.

 When a client asks you to plan a trip, what do you do?

 It depends on what the client wants. If she or he needs an airline ticket, the procedure is simple. We make at least three calls to find the best possible rate. If the client wants to rent a car or reserve a hotel room, we arrange those things, too.

 How do you and your colleagues at the agency split up the work?

 Everyone does everything, but each of us has special knowledge of certain places. My belief is that if I don't know something, somebody else does. We are a team and we depend on each other. On really large projects, two agents work together so that there is always someone to follow up if needed.

 How do you and your colleagues communicate?

 We hold daily meetings before the agency opens to talk about future concerns, discuss outside organizations we're using, and review any problems our clients have experienced.

Q **What tools do you depend on the most in your office?**

 A The telephone and the computer. We use them all the time. Everything we do for our clients goes into a computer database. We also rely on maps, timetables, and currency exchange charts.

 Q **Do you make out itineraries for your clients?**

A Every client gets an itinerary listing everything that has been arranged and paid for: car rentals, airline tickets, hotel rooms, and more. Every move the client will make is listed.

 Q **How do you communicate with organizations in other countries?**

A Fax machines are essential. If you call an organization in a foreign country, you might not reach anyone who speaks your language.

But if you send a fax, there is always someone who can translate. My colleagues speak a total of six different languages, so we can usually translate incoming faxes here in our office.

 Q **If you could travel anywhere in the world, where would you go?**

 A Every year I take a trip to a different place. This year I am going to Jordan.

Marie French's Tips for Group Travelers

1 Split up the research and planning for your trip.

2 If you're visiting a foreign country, learn a few words and phrases in the language of that country.

3 Take turns suggesting things to do. Don't be afraid to try new things.

4 Respect the culture and customs of the place you visit.

How to
Create a Travel Brochure

How can travelers figure out what to expect when visiting a new place? They might consult a travel brochure.

What is a travel brochure? A travel brochure is an illustrated booklet that describes a travel destination. It usually includes information on such topics as what to see and do, how to get around, where to eat, and where to stay. Travel brochures are found at tourist information centers and travel agencies.

Cheekwood
Tennessee Botanical Gardens and Museum of Art

Photos and maps appeal to a reader and show people what to expect on their visit.

Maps help visitors find their way to the destination.

This section gives at-a-glance information that's important to visitors.

THE PARTHENON

THE PARTHENON CENTENNIAL PARK

I 265

I 40

I 65

Charlotte Pk   Downtown

25th

West End-
Broadway

Harding Rd

I 65-I 40

I 440   I 65

I 24
I 40

Located only five minutes west of downtown Nashville, the Parthenon in Centennial Park is convenient to interstate highways, area colleges and universities, world famous Music Row and major retail and entertainment centers.

Most brochures include a few short paragraphs that give a brief history of the destination and tell what's particularly interesting or unique about it.

A well stocked, moderately priced gift shop is located in the main lobby of the Parthenon's gallery level entrance. With gifts and remembrances ranging from clothing to games, from jewelry to stationery, from original art to reproductions of Greek antiquities, the Parthenon Gift Shop is popular with Nashvillians and visitors alike.

H O U R S :
Tuesday - Saturday: 9 AM - 4:30 PM
Call for extended summer hours.

A D M I S S I O N S :
Adults (18-61): $2.50
Children and Seniors: $1.25
Group rates available on request.
Hours and admissions subject to change.

-THENON
al Park
N 37201
8431

rd of Parks
ation

N, MAYOR

THE SPIRIT LIVES ON

RYMAN
AUDITORIUM.sm

Nashville's Premier
Performance Hall & Museum

1 Choose a Destination

With your team, choose a destination for a brochure. Your brochure could be about a place (such as a city), a site (such as a park or a museum), or an event (such as a festival). Brainstorm places you've already visited or would like to visit. List some sites and events in your community that are interesting. Decide, as a team, which destination to write about.

TOOLS

• paper and pencil

• art supplies

2 Make Plans

Decide what sort of information should appear in your brochure. If you've chosen a site, for example, you'll need to find out when it's open and whether any special events are taking place there. You needn't stick to strictly factual data about your destination. Try to include a quote from a satisfied visitor or a mention of your own favorite thing to do there. Keep in mind that your goal is to make people want to visit the destination, as well as to give them the information they'll need once they arrive.

3 Gather Information

You and your teammates should work individually to gather information for your travel brochure. Decide which information each team member will find. You might also assign one person to find or draw pictures for the brochure.

To locate information and pictures, look at travel books and magazines, and the travel sections of newspapers. Encyclopedias and atlases are great sources of maps, charts and other data. If possible, you might also contact the visitors' bureau or chamber of commerce nearest your destination.

Tip If you're creating a brochure about a place you've already visited, you'll want to use any photos and information that you brought home from the trip.

4 Create a Brochure

Assemble your information and create your brochure! You might want to organize your information into categories with headings such as "Lodging," "Food," "Special Attractions," and "Maps." Put your information and illustrations together in brochure form. Think up a catchy title. When your brochure has been completed to the satisfaction of everyone on your team, present it to your class.

If You Are Using a Computer ...

Create your travel brochure on the computer. Use clip art to illustrate your work, or leave room for your own pictures.

THINK

How does your completed brochure represent the strengths or special interests of each teammate that worked on it?

Marie French
Travel Agent ▶

A successful journey is the result of a team effort.

Part of the Crew

Join an Inuit brother and sister as they learn survival skills.

Meet Darryl Roberts and his Icewalk teammates.

Follow along as three travel teammates document their journey to the Amazon.

WORKSHOP 2

Work with a team to plan a journey and write a travel itinerary.

Washington, D.C. Getaway

51

WINTER CAMP

It's winter, and John and Annie Laurie—known as Toughboy and Sister—are far away from their small Alaskan village. Their guardian, Natasha, has taken them to her winter trapping camp, where they will spend two months learning the "old ways"—trapping for food and clothing, chopping a water hole in the ice, and keeping warm in sub-zero temperatures. One of their first tasks is to quickly and carefully set traps before the bitter cold sets in.

By KIRKPATRICK HILL

Illustrated by SHONTO BEGAY

THE NEXT MORNING THEY GOT UP AT FIVE.
Now that their work around the cabin was finished, it was
time to set the lines.

Sister put the coffee on while Natasha made a pot of
oatmeal. They drank coffee and ate pilot crackers and stewed
prunes, and oatmeal with canned milk and brown sugar.

They hurried to do their chores. These had to be done
in the morning because they would be too tired at night.
Toughboy brought in the wood while Sister ran with the
buckets and the ice pick to the water hole. Natasha did the
dishes and swept the dirt floor.

Natasha filled their backpacks with the things they'd
need. There were number one marten traps and straw in
Toughboy's pack and the bait fish and tools in Natasha's. In
Sister's pack there were matches and their lunch. They each
would carry a little hatchet for clearing brush out of the trail.

They had to dress very carefully to spend the whole day
outdoors. Natasha watched how they put on their clothes.
They'd be far away from the cabin and couldn't come in
when they felt cold. They had to dress so they would
stay warm.

First there was their long underwear, which they slept
in. Over that their jeans and flannel shirts, and then their
snow pants, which each had a bib to cover their chests.
They must wear one pair of cotton socks and one pair of

wool socks. Socks must never be tight or their feet would get cold right away.

Sister wanted to wear her new mukluks, but it was still too warm. Mukluks had moose-hide bottoms, so they weren't any good if the snow was wet. They had to wear their shoepacks until it was colder.

They wore short jackets over the snow pants, and knitted wool caps.

On top of all that were the long canvas overparkas that Natasha had brought for them. These slipped over their heads and had big pockets in the front.

They would pull up the hood if the wind blew. The hoods had wolverine ruffs. Wolverine was the best kind of ruff because it didn't frost up in the cold like a wolf or a fox ruff.

They each wore a pair of cotton work gloves and over those a pair of big moose-hide mitts. The mitts were fastened to braided yarn harnesses that went around their necks, so the mitts could never be lost.

There were big yarn pom-poms on the harness pieces that went across the chest and at the ends of the harnesses, at the wrists.

When you didn't need them you tied the mittens behind your back, out of the way.

The backs of Natasha's mitts were made of otter and she'd sewn a beautiful wristband with inlaid pieces of fur. She had braided a red yarn harness for her mitts, and the pom-poms were as big around as teacups.

Sister wished she had a pair of mitts like that.

They started out at seven-thirty, and the moon, still bright, lit up the whole river. They walked slowly, chopping away the willows that had overgrown the trail.

Natasha had two lines, a long one and a short one. The long one was seven miles to the end, fourteen miles altogether. That was the one they were setting today.

When they came to the bend of the river the sun began to rise and the sky flooded with pink and purple light. Blue clouds floated in that brilliant sky and birds swooped and glided far ahead of them, as if they were drunk on the colors.

The river was wide there, and far away there were hills and miles and miles of spruce trees edging the river.

Sister thought how wonderful it was to be so far away from everything. It was so quiet.

Just then an angry sound ripped the silence, and far, far above them a tiny jet began to write a white line in the morning sky.

Even if you go as far away as you can, thought Sister, there will still be something to remind you of the big world outside all these trees. Even if you went to the middle of the desert in Australia there would be something.

It could never be the way it was in the old days.

NATASHA SHOWED THEM THE PLACES ON A SPRUCE tree where a porcupine had been gnawing. Porcupines could climb trees, she said. Lots of people didn't know that. If you couldn't catch anything else, sometimes people could catch porcupines because they move so slowly. "Don't need no gun, or nothing. Just club them with a stick. Good eating, too."

If they saw a scattering of spruce needles on the snow that would tell them that there was a spruce hen up in that tree, eating.

Every so often Natasha would stop and hack away some brush and there would be one of her old marten traps.

Toughboy didn't know how she knew where each one was. You couldn't see them at all as you were walking the trail. Natasha tied a bright pink surveyor's ribbon to a branch near each trap, because she said Toughboy would never be able to find the traps when she wasn't with him.

Natasha's traps were pole sets. A thin spruce pole was nailed at a slant against a tree. The trap was nailed by its chain to the place where the pole and the tree met, about four feet up the tree. The marten would run up the pole and step onto the trap.

If the old trap had broken or rusted she'd nail on one of the new traps from Toughboy's pack. She'd set the trap with a piece of the bait fish and cover it carefully with a little dried grass.

They saw a few rabbits, which still had dark patches in their fur. In a few weeks, when more snow had fallen, they would be all white. Natasha said some years the rabbits were everywhere, and in those years they would catch lots of lynx with wire snares.

She showed them how to whistle at a rabbit. If you whistle, that rabbit will stop right there and listen and you can get a good shot with your twenty-two.

Toughboy wished he'd see a rabbit so he could try the whistle. Then a big rabbit crashed through the willows right onto his path, but it was going too fast for Toughboy to even think about whistling at it. It had scared him so badly that his heart was nearly jumping out of his chest.

By the time they reached the end of the seven-mile line, Toughboy didn't think he could walk another step. He threw himself down in the snow at the side of the trail and stretched out his arms and legs. He stared at the blue sky and thought of his bunk at the cabin.

He had never walked so far before, and he felt as if he'd loosened his legs from their hip sockets. His heels hurt him and he wanted to take his boots off. And they still had to turn around and go back again.

He could tell Sister was tired, too. She stuck her tongue out like Mutt did when he had been running, to show him that she was worn out.

They looked at Natasha, who was over seventy. Maybe nearly eighty. She didn't look even a little bit tired.

Natasha told Sister to get the dry meat and pilot crackers out of her pack. "Look," she said to Toughboy. "I'll show you how to make a fire on the trail."

Toughboy wished she'd just make the fire herself and let him lie there, but he didn't say so.

She showed Toughboy the little gray branches under a tiny spruce tree. "Anywhere you have these spruce trees, underneath there's these little dry twigs. You can use that to start a fire anytime."

They each gathered a handful from the little trees by the side of the trail, and then Natasha chopped up some dead willow branches with her hatchet. She put a match to the little pile of spruce tinder and when it was flaming she added the dry wood. In no time there was a nice little fire.

She took a one-pound coffee can from Sister's pack and filled it with snow. She set the can in the fire, and when the water was boiling she added tea.

She poured the tea into the three tin mugs from Sister's pack and got out the jar of sugar, and they had the best lunch anyone could imagine, sitting right there at the end of the trail in the snow.

After drinking tea Toughboy felt as if he could walk again. But he didn't think he'd ever be as tough as Natasha. Or the old-timers. He didn't even think he cared, he was so tired.

That night Toughboy and Sister didn't eat any dinner. After they'd hung up their clothes to dry, they lay on their bunks and were asleep in seconds. They slept so hard it felt as if they had been sleeping just minutes when Natasha woke them up the next morning.

THE NEXT DAY THEY WERE GOING to set the short line. Toughboy was glad they would only be walking eight miles that day, instead of fourteen.

When she saw how relieved he looked, Natasha jeered, "Don't get happy. The short line goes up two hills, so it's harder than the long line."

Toughboy couldn't imagine anything harder than the long line. His legs were sore and stiff. He almost groaned out loud when he sat down to pull his wool socks on. Why didn't Natasha get sore? Old-time people must be made tougher, he could see that.

Natasha said you had to check your traps every other day. If you left the fur in the trap for longer than a day the shrews might chew on it and ruin the skin. Only lazy trappers let their fur get ruined.

They would walk the short line one day, and the long line the next.

Natasha said that three people were better than two and two were better than one, because it was very hard for just one person to trap. There was too much for one person to do.

There was so much work every day, Sister didn't see how they would ever have done their schoolwork if they'd brought it. And she would not have had time to read those books, either.

The old-time people didn't have time to go to school very much. And when they were out of school they didn't have time to do anything but work, work, work all their lives. Working to stay warm, and working to stay fed.

And when they'd used up all their time doing both of those things, there wasn't any time left to do anything else. Sister liked to work, but she wanted time to do something besides that. She didn't know what, exactly, but she'd know someday.

As they walked along the short line Natasha would stop at the grass lakes and sloughs and creeks to teach them about the ice.

Grass lakes were shallow ponds full of marsh grass, and so the water froze differently there than the water in creeks. Sloughs were branches of the river and their ice was different from the ice on the river or the creeks or the grass lakes.

Every day the ice would change with the weather. You had to know what you were looking at and what the sounds of the ice meant.

You had to know where the swift places in the river were, because the ice would always be dangerous there.

You must test the ice with a stick or your ice pick, and listen for the dull sound of sturdy ice.

There might be an open place in the river and a thin layer of ice would form over that water. Then it would snow on top of that and you would think there was thick ice under that snow. Lots of people drowned that way. You had to learn to read the signs on the snow cover, and to be careful.

After it had snowed and you couldn't see the ice anymore, you had to be careful of overflow. That was the most dangerous thing of all. Water would ooze out of cracks in the ice when there was a heavy snow or if it got very cold or very warm all of a sudden. The slush would lie under the snow and you couldn't see it.

Sometimes snow machines or airplanes would get stuck in the overflow. They would freeze into that slush right away, and it would take a lot of work to get them out again. That's why Billy had dragged his skis on the ice before he landed.

If you stepped in overflow you'd get your boots wet and then your feet might freeze. Natasha said if their boots got wet through, they must stop and make a fire right away and take off their shoepacks or mukluks and socks and get them dry before they went on. She knew a lot of people who had frozen their feet trying to get home first. If your feet were badly frozen they might have to be cut off in the hospital.

"Why don't we always carry extra socks and mukluks in our packs?" asked Sister. "Then we'd always be safe, and we wouldn't even have to make a fire."

Natasha looked disgusted. "You don't get ready for a bad thing to happen. You just make it happen that way. That will give you bad luck."

That seemed very silly to Sister.

They were on the ridge near the end of the short trail when a huge owl flew along ahead of them as if it were guiding them. Its wings nearly touched the trees on both sides of the trail, it was so big. It glided and swooped ahead of them for nearly a mile, silent.

Natasha finally stopped on the trail and talked to it in Indian. Then it flew off the trail and left them, as if she'd told it to go away.

Owls could speak in Indian, but when they did they would tell you something bad. Maybe somebody would be going to die or an accident was going to happen. This owl didn't say anything, but still it had made Natasha nervous, the way it just flew along ahead of them. Owls knew too much.

Ravens were different. When ravens flew above them their wings were noisy, beating the sky like laundry flapping in the wind.

Toughboy and Sister loved to listen to the ravens. They had so many voices, you could never tell which one they would use. Sometimes they cried *bonk, bonk,* like hollow drums, and sometimes they screeched in a horrible way that made Toughboy and Sister laugh.

Natasha said when you were out hunting, the ravens would make a certain sound to tell you if there was a moose or caribou nearby. They would help you out if they felt like it. Toughboy and Sister thought that ravens weren't serious enough to give much good advice.

EVERY NIGHT, AS SOON AS THEY CAME into the cabin, they had to take care of their clothes. No matter how tired they were. That was the most important thing to learn at the trapline. If you didn't take care of your clothes the right way you might freeze your feet or hands.

First you had to put your boots by the fire to dry. You took out the felt liners and hung them and your wool socks on the clothesline over the stove with clothespins. Socks and liners had to be perfectly dry when you put them into your boots in the morning. You could freeze your feet if they were damp.

Then you had to take the gloves out of your moose-hide mittens and hang both the mittens and gloves up there over the heat. Your snow pants and your parka and your over-parka and your scarf and your hat all had to be hung up, too.

Toughboy and Sister had to stand on a stool to do this, and it seemed to take forever. Toughboy was always half-disgusted by the time he was through. But in the morning when he got dressed again, it was a good feeling to put on all those warm dry clothes.

Over the stove and behind the stove the lines were always full of drying clothes. Sister hated that because they made the cabin look untidy. As soon as the things were dry she'd hang them back on their nails by the door.

SOURCE

ACTION

Magazine

AWARD
WINNING

Magazine

Trail of

The Journey of Darryl Roberts

Courage

DARRYL ROBERTS sat in the tent. He checked his right foot.

His toenails were falling off. The skin on his heel was gone. It looked like it had been cut away with a knife.

Walking in the deadly cold had destroyed Darryl's feet. He had frostbite. He had blisters. And he had hundreds of miles left to walk. His goal: to walk to the North Pole. And he wasn't about to give up.

"I didn't want to put on my skis in the morning but I did," Darryl said. "I knew that for the next 14 hours I was going to feel horrible pain. Sometimes it felt like my feet were breaking in two. I just kept on walking."

For Darryl, age 23, the trip was a brutal challenge. To get to the Pole, he and seven other men walked 500 miles in 56 days. Each man carried 100 pounds of supplies over the ice-covered Arctic Ocean. The team had little rest. There were many dangers.

"We carried a rifle in case we were attacked by hungry polar bears or wolves. Luckily, we didn't run into any," Darryl said. "We also had to worry about the temperature. At 70 degrees below zero, you can get serious frostbite. You can lose fingers and toes. It's a scary feeling."

Another danger was the ice. "Sometimes the ice would move around. Other times it was too thin," Darryl said. "One time the ice moved right under my skis. My heart jumped. I thought someone was going to fall through and die."

The team faced other tests as well. To survive, the eight men slept in one tiny, uncomfortable tent. And every day they ate the same thing: dried cereal, powdered milk, and *muktuk*. Muktuk is dried whale fat. It is a common food in the Arctic.

An icewalker crosses a treacherous crack in the ice.

Sometimes Darryl missed the comforts of home. "I thought about how nice it would be to stay home and call out for a pizza!"

Darryl lost 13 pounds during his long, hard march. But that was the least of his problems. Darryl's biggest challenge were his feet. Every step was a painful struggle.

At one point, team members wanted him to quit and go home. Darryl refused. He was determined to go on. "He showed real courage," said one teammate. "It's tough enough to reach the North Pole when you're healthy. For Darryl, to make it suffering from frostbite was incredible."

Darryl learned about courage from his mother. She left high school to raise Darryl and his brother. She raised them alone. But she never gave up.

"My mother went back and got her high school diploma. Then she went to college," Darryl said. "I saw how hard she worked. And I knew with hard work I could make *anything* happen."

Why did Darryl go to the North Pole? "I walked there to prove I could face any challenge," Darryl said. "But I also had another reason," he added. "I come from a tough neighborhood. It's a place where kids face problems. The problems are as tough as reaching the North Pole. I thought of these kids as I walked," Darryl said. "I wanted to prove to them that if I can meet my challenge, they can meet theirs, too."

The members of the Icewalk team assemble for a group portrait.

ICEWALK TEAM

Robert Swan

Rupert Summerson

Graeme Joy

Mikhail Malachov

Angus Clance Cockney

Hiroshi Onishi

Arved Fuchs

Darryl Roberts

Among them, the eight members of the Icewalk team shared many years of hiking and mountain climbing expertise. Each member of the team also brought his own unique skill and talent to the expedition. Meet the team members:

Expedition leader Robert Swan of the United Kingdom organized Icewalk and became the first person in history to walk to both poles.

Hiroshi Onishi of Japan brought ten years of experience as a mountaineer, hiker, and climber. Onishi is a full-time expeditioner.

A geologist and an expert on the Arctic, Rupert Summerson of Great Britain was the navigator for Icewalk. He was also responsible for conducting scientific experiments.

Team doctor Mikhail Malachov of Russia brought his expertise in winter expeditions and frostbite.

Canoe expeditionist Arved Fuchs of the former West Germany had reached the magnetic North Pole in a collapsible canoe on a prior trip in 1985.

Geography teacher Graeme Joy of Australia has a reputation as one of Australia's top marathon kayak racers.

Canadian Angus Clance Cockney, an Inuk (a native of the Arctic), contributed his skills as a champion cross-country skier and coach.

The youngest member of the team, Darryl Roberts of the United States, trained young people from New York City in cross-country skiing, orienteering, and backpacking.

From

AMAZON

By Peter Lourie – Photographs by Marcos Santilli

Traveling to any new location is a challenge, but when your purpose is to document your journey, the need for cooperation is more important than ever. Writer Peter Lourie, photographer Marcos Santilli, and Marcos's wife, Marlui, a sound specialist, set out to bring the story of the rain forest to the rest of the world. Their journey took them to Rondônia, a state in eastern Brazil.

Peter Lourie, Marcos Santilli, and Marlui travel through Rondônia atop a coal car.

Before I left for the Amazon, I pinned a huge map of South America on my wall. For hours I'd stare at the big green heart of the continent, wondering what I'd find when I got there. I was headed for the Brazilian state of Rondônia.

The year before my trip to the Amazon, I met Marcos Santilli, a top Brazilian photographer. He had come to New York City to raise money for another expedition into the rain forest. He said I should come with him to witness for myself what was happening to the jungle. How could I refuse? As a writer I love to travel to places and write about them.

Marcos had first traveled to the Amazon years before. Shocked by what he found, he decided to return with his wife to document the devastation of the rain forest. The following year he and his wife Marlui spent a few months in Rondônia. Marcos set off early each morning and again in the late afternoon to catch the good light for his photographs. Marlui, a musician, recorded the many sounds of the jungle. She also collected the songs of the rubber tappers, gold miners, and Indians.

In the late summer of 1981, I joined their team. Our trip was a collaboration between a photographer, a writer, and a sound specialist. I brought notebooks and a small tape recorder to use for my interviews, and I learned some Portuguese. I flew to the capital city of Rondônia called Porto Velho and met Marcos and Marlui in August.

A week later we set out from Porto Velho. At the end of the highway we would leave the Jeep and hire a small boat to motor up a little-traveled river. Here we hoped to reach a tribe of Indians in the uncut jungle before the old way of life vanished.

When I returned from my trip to the Amazon, I wrote a book based on my experiences and used many of Marcos's photographs. You are about to read a section of that book which is about our trip through Rondônia and the Indians we met. I often recall what I learned and the fun we had traveling as a team exploring a wilderness and meeting fascinating people. Enjoy the book!

Peter Lourie

A section of rain forest that has been cut and is burning

THE ROAD AND THE FIRE

We traveled in my friends' Jeep along what is known simply as the BR-364, a dirt road that had been cut like a long scar through the middle of Rondônia. The road was in terrible condition with ruts and potholes the size of elephants.

It is amazing how fast the rain forest can turn to dust when the thick, green jungle is cut and burned. Along the road going south from the capital, the colonists had cleared thousands and thousands of acres for farms and pastures. The area was so dry that the violet dust rose into the air and covered absolutely everything. Our camera equipment, our hair, and our skin were layered with the fine Rondônian dust. It clogged our nostrils and made it hard to breathe.

The state of Rondônia, an area about the size of Wyoming, or twice the size of England, was entirely jungle a few decades ago.

But now much of it has been turned into towns and a network of roads. Colonists have been flooding into the state since the 1970s, when the government of Brazil began encouraging people to move here. Rondônia is just one of the Amazon states colonized by hundreds of thousands of people looking for a better life. Families arrive in the Amazon from all parts of Brazil. They come from regions of drought and famine, they come from over-crowded cities, and they hope to find Paradise here in the jungle. Sometimes four or five families will come in one run-down old truck, which is like the covered wagon of the American West. Brazilians call these trucks "Macaws' Perches" because they have very narrow, hard wooden seats. And they carry all the colonists' belongings, which are as colorful as tropical birds: all their chickens, pigs, furniture, pets, and clothes—everything.

Although the colonists are seeking a good life, they often find it very hard in Amazonia. They are threatened by rampant diseases like malaria. And the land is difficult to farm. When settlers first arrive, they cut and burn the jungle so they can begin to grow crops like coffee and cacao. Unfortunately, after only a few years these kinds of crops deplete the delicate jungle soil, and soon the land grows so dry it turns to a near desert. And the colonists move on.

Fires burning in Rondônia during the dry season

The fastest way to get rid of the jungle is to cut and burn it during the dry months of August and September. We traveled during this dry season and saw so many fires burning along the roads that the sky had turned to a blue haze.

This colonization of the Amazon is much like what happened in the American West in the 1800s. When the West was settled, railroads were built, buffalo were killed, and the prairies were cultivated. But what took eighty years to accomplish in the United States will take far fewer years in the Amazon with bulldozers and other modern machinery. The Amazon basin, with its network of hundreds and hundreds of rivers, was inaccessible for ages. This huge area (the basin is a little smaller than the continental United States) supplies a fifth of the earth's fresh water and includes one third of its tropical rain forest. But the wilderness is vanishing quickly. Perhaps colonization is necessary in a modern world, and Brazil is following in the footsteps of many other nations. But the planet will lose these precious few remaining rain forests with the coming of civilization.

Today many scientists believe that loss of the jungle means we will lose fauna and flora that have not yet been studied.

The Amazon harbors many thousand species of plants and many million animal and insect species, an estimated one-fifth of all the world's bird species, and perhaps eight times as many kinds of fish as in the Mississippi River and its tributaries. Some scientists are also worried about the carbon dioxide produced from all the fires burning in the Amazon. They fear this will add to the layer of carbon dioxide and other gases from burning fossil fuels. Although burning the rain forests contributes much less than automobile emissions, the accumulated carbon forms a layer of gas, scientists believe, that prevents too little of the warmth created from the sun's rays from escaping back into space. This heat then builds up and creates what is known as the Greenhouse Effect, which some scientists fear might lead to excessive global warming.

We followed the road farther south through more and more burning jungle. As we approached the fires, the air got hotter and hotter until it was too hot to take pictures. We wanted to get back to the cool river. We'd seen too much burning and too many people destroying ancient jungle. So we decided to visit an Indian tribe in a part of Rondônia still untouched by the colonists.

63°

Fires like these are responsible for the build-up of carbon dioxide
that causes the Greenhouse Effect.

Children play in a small tributary of the Mamoré River.

INDIANS

My friends and I rented a small boat with only a canvas tarp as a roof. We went for miles on a small tributary of the Mamoré River, which was very narrow in places. Clusters of tangled palm trees hung over the banks. It seemed as if no one had ever been up this river before. There were no houses here, no television, no roads, and no colonists—at least not yet. We could tell the rainy season was coming. Each day it rained a little more. Huge rain clouds formed and dissolved over the great forest. After a few days' travel, we reached the Indian outpost. Dusk was falling quickly, and the frogs on shore began to croak.

These Indians were far enough away from civilization that they could live much like they had for centuries. But even here certain changes had come. The children were not learning the old customs. They could not sing the old tribal songs. The elders found this sad. Marlui, who had brought her guitar, sang a song of her own. The children sat around her and sang songs that the missionaries had taught them.

The high point of our visit was the fishing trip. More than thirty of us walked through a flurry of butterflies by the thousands until we came to a small river in a clearing. When we reached a place where the river formed a natural pool, the boys went into the jungle to look for lianas from a timbó tree. They dragged the long, snakelike lianas back to the river and cut them into pieces a few feet long. They waded into the water and beat the wood together hard and fast. From the splintering fibers, a natural poison spread out into the pool.

In about an hour, when the chemical had taken effect, the fish began to float to the surface. Most of them were stunned but not yet dead. With bare hands the boys and girls scooped up the fish and tossed them onto the beach. Other children laughed and gathered the fish in piles. Some used bows and arrows to spear the fish that had not yet floated to the surface.

We were witnesses to the old Indian life, the life that had been going on here for thousands of years. But having seen the road and the fires of the burning jungle not far away, we knew this life and the peace of the jungle would be shattered forever. There would be the sound of chain saws in the forest and the sound of the roaring jungle in flames.

A young boy looks over the hazy rain forest.

Perhaps there would be no more plants that made the chemical needed to stun the fish. And this kind of simple fishing trip might soon disappear.

The next day we got back into our boat. The Indians waved good-bye. The sky was clearing. The strong winds from the Andes that preceded the heavy rains were wiping away the smoke and dust from the roads in the South. The dry season was ending and the mud season was on its way.

We had seen the untouched Amazon and the invasion of urban civilization. We had seen tribal life and the isolated life of the rubber tapper. We had seen the Devil's Railroad and the camp of the hard-living gold miners. Most striking perhaps was our impression of the burning rain forest. Those fires seemed to have burned images of flame and smoke into our hearts.

Now as we left the tribal outpost and headed back the way we had come, we glided downriver with the soft, slow, ancient current. There was something moving in the river—something playful and magic breaking the water's calm. There they were! Five porpoises rose and dove and swam around our boat as if to say good-bye forever.

How to Develop an Itinerary

Itineraries indicate ●••
the length of the trip.

The places visited on ●•
the tour appear at
the top of the
itinerary.

Each day is described ●
in detail.

Successful travel requires teamwork and planning. Time spent working with others to develop an itinerary helps to make a trip safe and enjoyable.

What is an itinerary? An itinerary is a plan or an outline for a trip. Itineraries can range from one typed page to a four-color brochure. Itineraries usually detail day-by-day activities, such as where the travelers will go, what they will see, and where they will stay.

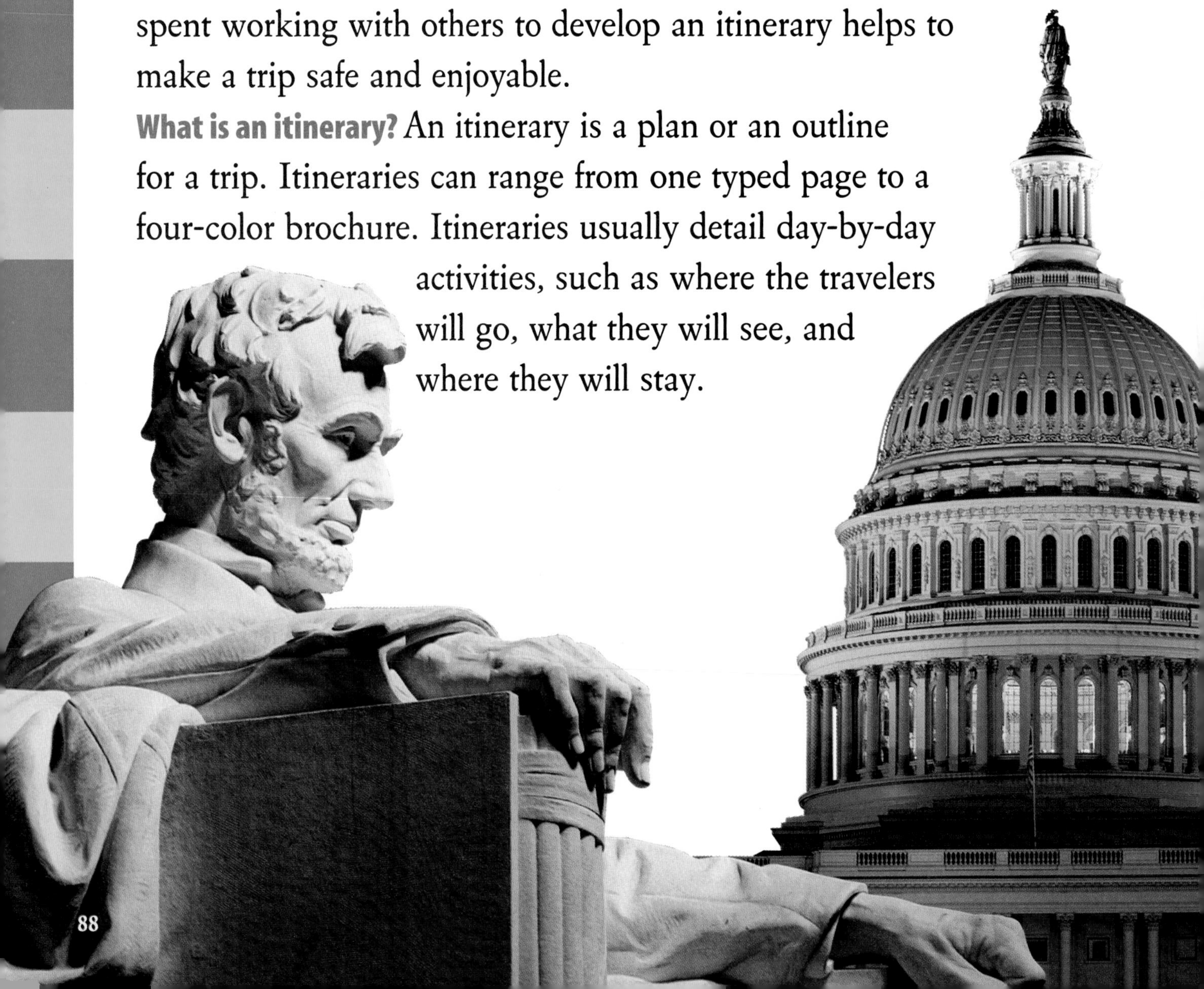

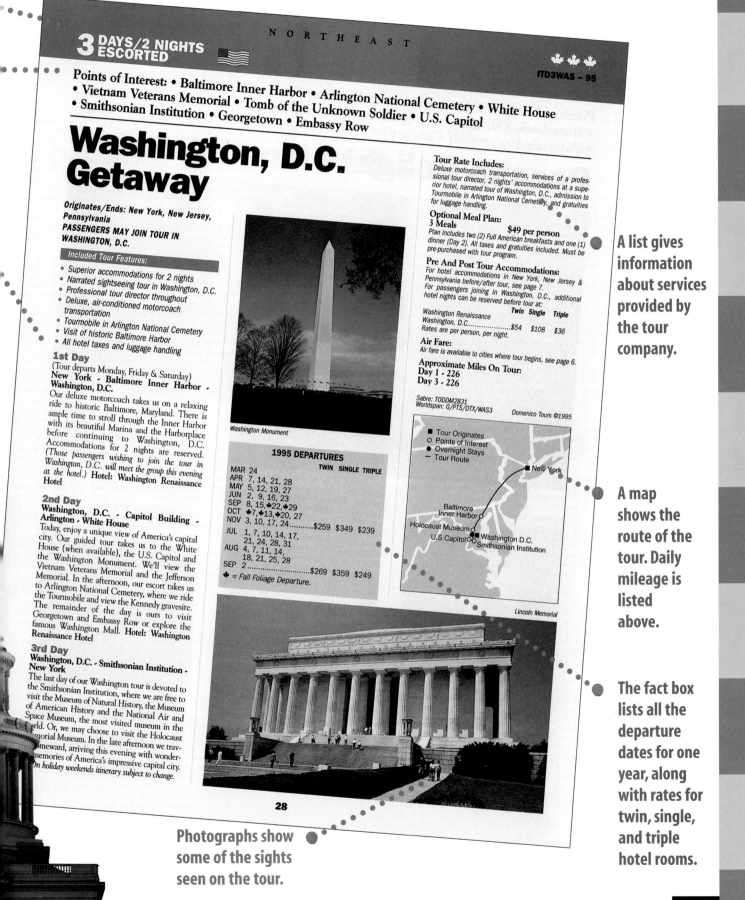

3 DAYS/2 NIGHTS ESCORTED

ITD3WAS – 95

Points of Interest: • Baltimore Inner Harbor • Arlington National Cemetery • White House • Vietnam Veterans Memorial • Tomb of the Unknown Soldier • U.S. Capitol • Smithsonian Institution • Georgetown • Embassy Row

Washington, D.C. Getaway

Originates/Ends: New York, New Jersey, Pennsylvania
PASSENGERS MAY JOIN TOUR IN WASHINGTON, D.C.

Included Tour Features:

- Superior accommodations for 2 nights
- Narrated sightseeing tour in Washington, D.C.
- Professional tour director throughout
- Deluxe, air-conditioned motorcoach transportation
- Tourmobile in Arlington National Cemetery
- Visit of historic Baltimore Harbor
- All hotel taxes and luggage handling

1st Day

(Tour departs Monday, Friday & Saturday)
New York - Baltimore Inner Harbor - Washington, D.C.
Our deluxe motorcoach takes us on a relaxing ride to historic Baltimore, Maryland. There is ample time to stroll through the Inner Harbor with its beautiful Marina and the Harborplace before continuing to Washington, D.C. Accommodations for 2 nights are reserved. (Those passengers wishing to join the tour in Washington, D.C. will meet the group this evening at the hotel.) **Hotel: Washington Renaissance Hotel**

2nd Day

Washington, D.C. - Capitol Building - Arlington - White House
Today, enjoy a unique view of America's capital city. Our guided tour takes us to the White House (when available), the U.S. Capitol and the Washington Monument. We'll view the Vietnam Veterans Memorial and the Jefferson Memorial. In the afternoon, our escort takes us to Arlington National Cemetery, where we ride the Tourmobile and view the Kennedy gravesite. The remainder of the day is ours to visit Georgetown and Embassy Row or explore the famous Washington Mall. **Hotel: Washington Renaissance Hotel**

3rd Day

Washington, D.C. - Smithsonian Institution - New York
The last day of our Washington tour is devoted to the Smithsonian Institution, where we are free to visit the Museum of Natural History, the Museum of American History and the National Air and Space Museum, the most visited museum in the world. Or, we may choose to visit the Holocaust Memorial Museum. In the late afternoon we travel homeward, arriving this evening with wonderful memories of America's impressive capital city. On holiday weekends itinerary subject to change.

Washington Monument

Tour Rate Includes:

Deluxe motorcoach transportation, services of a professional tour director, 2 nights' accommodations at a superior hotel, narrated tour of Washington, D.C., admission to Tourmobile in Arlington National Cemetery, and gratuities for luggage handling.

Optional Meal Plan:

3 Meals $49 per person
Plan includes two (2) Full American breakfasts and one (1) dinner (Day 2). All taxes and gratuities included. Must be pre-purchased with tour program.

Pre And Post Tour Accommodations:

For hotel accommodations in New York, New Jersey & Pennsylvania before/after tour, see page 7. For passengers joining in Washington, D.C., additional hotel nights can be reserved before tour at:

	Twin	Single	Triple
Washington Renaissance Washington, D.C.	$54	$108	$36

Rates are per person, per night.

Air Fare:

Air fare is available to cities where tour begins, see page 6.

Approximate Miles On Tour:

Day 1 - 226
Day 3 - 226

Sabre: TODDM2831
Worldspan: G/PTS/DTX/WAS3

Domenico Tours ©1995

■ Tour Originates
○ Points of Interest
● Overnight Stays
— Tour Route

New York
Baltimore Inner Harbor
Holocaust Museum
U.S. Capitol   Washington D.C.   Smithsonian Institution

1995 DEPARTURES

		TWIN	SINGLE	TRIPLE
MAR	24			
APR	7, 14, 21, 28			
MAY	5, 12, 19, 27			
JUN	2, 9, 16, 23			
SEP	8, 15,♣22,♣29			
OCT	♣7,♣13,♣20, 27			
NOV	3, 10, 17, 24	$259	$349	$239
JUL	1, 7, 10, 14, 17, 21, 24, 28, 31			
AUG	4, 7, 11, 14, 18, 21, 25, 28			
SEP	♣ 2	$269	$359	$249

♣ = Fall Foliage Departure.

Lincoln Memorial

28

89

1 Brainstorm

Where would you go, and what would you do, if you could go anywhere in the world? With your team, choose a destination for a week's vacation. You can stay in one place or visit several spots. Decide what sort of vacation activity you'd like to focus on. Will you visit a theme park? take a ski trip? tour museums or historic sites? backpack through the wilderness?

Remember, you have only seven days to complete your travel!

TOOLS

- paper and pencil
- folder
- photographs and maps
- art supplies

2 Divide the Work

Make a list of the questions you'll need to answer to put together your travel itinerary. Depending on the size of your team, assign each team member to research one or two items. Your list will probably include questions such as the following:

- Transportation: How do we get from place to place?

- Recreation and sightseeing: What can we do at each place?

- Dining: Where do we eat?

- Lodging: Where do we sleep?

  - Weather: What is the best time of the year for this trip?

  - Budget: How much will the trip cost?

3 Research

Research the questions on your list. There are many sources of information about world destinations. You might want to try some of these:

- atlases and encyclopedias
- travel sections of libraries
- state tourist boards
- travel magazines
- travel sections of newspapers
- travel agencies or the Automobile Association of America
- other people who have traveled to your location

Take notes on the information you find. File them in a folder.

Tip Communication among team members is essential. For instance, your "transportation director" must be in touch with your "sightseeing planner" in order to arrange transportation to each sight you'll visit.

4 Complete Your Plans

Gather your research information. Use it to make group decisions about your trip: what forms of transportation you'll use, where you'll stay, how you'll spend each day, and what you'll do about meals.

Write your itinerary. Check it to make sure you haven't left out any times, dates, or other important details. Add any maps, charts, or illustrations you want to include.

Share your itinerary with your class. Would you like to trade your team's vacation for any of the others?

If You Are Using a Computer ...

Create a separate journal entry for each item you need to research. Record the information you find and share it with others on-line.

THINK

What kind of planning is involved when you take a class trip?

Marie French
Travel Agent ▶

Teams solve problems when they travel.

Thinking it Through

Meet a traveler of long ago, who's having a ship built for a dangerous journey.

Join Rich Wilson and his crew as they meet a challenge at sea.

Read a classic poem about the joys of traveling the seas.

PROJECT

Experience the rewards of teaming up to publish your own travel magazine.

TERRIFIC TRAVEL

In this issue:
Top Ten Dream Vacations
Page 10

93

David Macaulay

Historical
Novel

from

SHIP

by David Macaulay

In SHIP, *a fictional team of underwater archaeologists has been recovering and studying artifacts from a sunken caravel— a type of small wooden sailing ship. Then, one member of the team discovers an early-sixteenth-century journal that describes in detail the building of a caravel. The following journal entries tell how the main body of the ship was built and launched.*

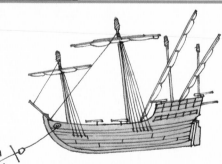

The Seventh day of January in the Year of Our Lord — 1504

Although my brother Garcia and I are presently enjoying great success importing dyewood and pearls from the Indies, it seems only prudent to be searching for new sources of these precious commodities before we run out (or someone else finds them). We have therefore commissioned the building of a caravel. Such a ship, although quite small, is surprisingly capacious. It is also of modest draft and can be heavily armed, making it ideal for the uncertainties of exploration.

This latest addition to the Vergara fleet is to be built by the Guerra shipyard, which continues to flourish under the watchful eye of the widow Guerra. Prices remain high, but so too does the quality of the work, all of which is overseen by master shipwright Alonso de Fonseca. Because my personal life in Seville has grown somewhat complicated, Garcia has agreed that I should sail with the ship on its maiden voyage. For my own piece of mind, therefore, I have taken it upon myself to observe and record all aspects of the vessel's construction.

The Ninth day of January

Master Alonso looks favorably upon my quest and promises that no detail shall be overlooked. We passed this rainy afternoon reviewing the list of timbers required for the hull, all of which, I am pleased to report, will be the finest white oak. Once a year, Alonso and his master carpenter, José de Arbora, visit the forests to select lumber for their ships. In the winter, the trees they have marked are felled and sent on their way.

The Eleventh day of January

Alonso, José and I passed much of this morning with two lumber merchants who were attempting to justify their high prices. They complained incessantly about the difficulty of transporting wood to the city. Alonso countered their claims by suggesting that the Guadalquivir River does all the work. "It flows directly from the mountains to the sea and passes right by our shipyard on its way. All you have to do is throw the logs in and, two hundred miles later, pull them out!"

The Eighteenth day of January

By the time I reached the yard, José and his able apprentices were already shaping the keel—the very backbone of our ship, which, incidentally, we have named *Magdalena*. "Once the rough shape has been established with the ax," he informed me, "each face of the timber will be smoothed with the short strokes of the adze." José is reputed to be one of the finest adze men in the city, although his apprenticeship was not without personal cost. His right foot carries only four toes.

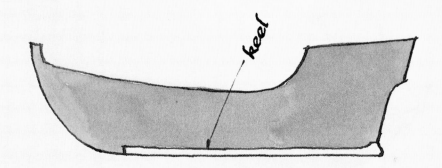

The Thirtieth day of January

Not surprisingly, my arrival this morning was greeted with greater than usual enthusiasm. As the sun, which has been rare of late, added its blessing to that of the good friar, *Magdalena*'s finished keel was levered up and onto its supports. This event, according to our contract, marks the day upon which my brother and I are bound to pay the first of three sums of money to the shipyard. This we did at the inn, in the presence of Alonso and the Señora's eldest son, Diego. After toasting the continued success of our venture, Master Alonso bade me accompany him to the blacksmith's. There he ordered large quantities of iron nails and bolts as well as two dozen spikes almost the length of my arm.

The Fifteenth day of February

The curved stempost that will lead *Magdalena* through the waves is now secured to the keel. A generous coating of pitch was applied to the adjoining surfaces before they were permanently fastened—a procedure that, Alonso assures me, will be repeated throughout construction to prevent rot. This afternoon a large curved brace called a deadwood was hoisted onto the keel where it fit with perfection into the curve of the stempost.

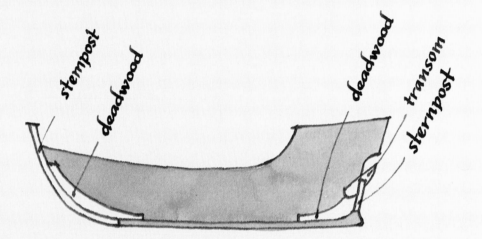

The Twenty-ninth day of February

The yard is very busy these days, and Alonso has been much distracted. One of Their Royal Highnesses' ships has been hauled over onto its side for repairs to the hull, and the cargo vessel that sits next to *Magdalena* is already being caulked in preparation for its launch. At the opposite end of *Magdalena*'s keel from the stempost, the sternpost and its deadwood are now in place. Together they support a fine broad transom. As I was leaving the yard, I found Alonso threatening one of the lumber merchants with all manner of legal retribution if the merchant did not immediately provide the promised timbers. "Did the Lord create lumber merchants simply to impede the shipwright's progress?" he shouted. "It is truly a miracle that Noah finished his work in time and that we were not all lost to the Great Flood."

The First day of March

From *Magdalena*'s sturdy spine, her ribs must now be built. After making a series of complicated calculations, which, he tells me, all begin with the length of the keel, Alonso creates two patterns from which all the largest ribs will be traced. Every rib is to be built in three pieces. The bottommost section, called the floor, will sit directly on the keel or deadwoods. Secured to the ends of each floor are the futtocks, which will support the sides of the ship. By slightly adjusting the pieces of the pattern for each one, Alonso and his apprentices trace the shapes of the first thirteen ribs.

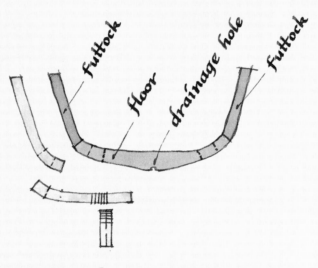

The Twentieth day of March

It has been some time since I put pen to paper. I was confined to my bed for two weeks with a terrible fever, although now, thanks be to God, I have regained my strength. Much has happened in my absence. The cargo ship that once stood next to *Magdalena* has been launched and now awaits its masts. Not only is our vessel free from its shadow, but the first of *Magdalena*'s ribs have been assembled and hoisted into place on the keel.

Because all ships, even those built by Alonso de Fonseca, are bound to leak, he has instructed that a small notch be cut at the base of each floor to direct water to the pump. I can tell you, having personally ventured into the holds of ships where this refinement was overlooked, the result is a most foul-smelling stew.

The Twenty-second day of March

This morning Alonso, José, and two apprentices began tacking thin strips of wood called ribbands between the posts and ribs on one side of the ship. Only after several hours of adjusting and readjusting did the two master craftsmen seem satisfied with the resulting shape. The curvature of each ribband was then carefully measured so that it could be replicated exactly on the opposite side of the ship. When all the ribbands are in place, a pattern will be made for each remaining rib.

The Twenty-fourth day of March

The keelson, an impressive piece of timber, is now installed. It rests upon the ribs directly above the keel. Because of its size and great weight, it was slipped into the hull before all the futtocks were attached.

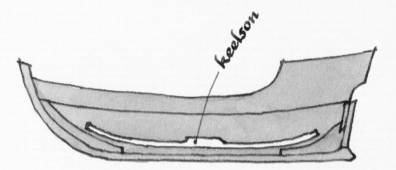

Easter Week

When the last of the ribs are in place, the tops of each futtock are then tied together by two heavy planks called wales. Each wale has been slowly bent over a hot fire so that it follows the curvature of the hull. Starting at the stempost on one side of the ship, carpenters move along the scaffolding, first drilling holes and then securing each connection with both iron nails and wooden pegs called treenails. It is José's desire to install both wales before the Easter fair, since leaving only one in place, even for a week, could cause the entire frame to become twisted.

The Twenty-fourth day of April

The keelson is notched to fit snugly over every floor and is held in place with long iron spikes. The wooden skeleton is further secured by two additional pieces of timber called stringers. These, too, are notched and extend from bow to stern along both sides of the keelson.

The Twenty-seventh day of April

Garcia chided me today for spending too much time at the shipyard. We have three ships leaving within the month, and there are still contracts to be drawn up and supplies to be gathered. I can barely force myself to confront the endless columns of figures that cover the pages of our ledgers, but as my elder brother points out, it is those endless columns which are paying for my current pleasure.

The Twenty-ninth day of April

It appears that Alonso has finally conquered the lumber men. Wood arrives every day, and much of it is immediately dragged to the saw pits for cutting. Piles of planks now lay waiting along both sides of the ship. José's carpenters have been sheathing the hull below the wales. They painstakingly measure and trim each plank to create the tightest possible seam before drilling and securing it to the ribs.

The Twenty-eighth day of May

Curved beams required to support the deck and ensure its drainage are now in place. José has begun framing a large hatch in the center of the deck so that cargo can be easily stored below. To increase the amount of deck space and provide some protection from the elements, a second, smaller deck is under construction at the stern.

The Thirty-first day of May

I was introduced today to Vincente Albene, a master caulker. He and his crew will seal the hull and later the deck by pounding strands of tar-soaked hemp called oakum into every seam. As a further precaution against leakage, Master Alonso has asked that a thin strip of lead be tacked over the oakum in those seams which will lie below the water line. No matter how well Albene does his work, however, some water will most certainly find its way into the hold. To return it to the sea as quickly as possible, Alonso has installed a pump that rises from the depths of the hold up through the main deck.

The Twenty-third day of June

The past two days have been spent getting ready for the launch. Once Albene and Alonso were satisfied with the caulking, the hull was coated with pitch. *Magdalena* was then carefully lowered onto two parallel wooden tracks that extend to the river. Tomorrow they will be covered with a thick coating of animal fat to help the ship slide more easily. The keel will travel freely in a trench dug between the tracks. This afternoon Alonso supervised the placement of many stones on the floor of the hold to help steady the ship as it enters the water.

The Twenty-fourth day of June

At about two o'clock Alonso gave the order from the bow to remove the remaining supports. At first there was no movement. Then, as people along both sides gently rocked the hull, it gradually slid onto the greased portion of the tracks. Cheers filled the air as the ship glided whole into the same river that only a few months earlier had delivered her in pieces.

The OCEAN

*I*n 1853 a big clipper ship named Northern Light *sailed from San Francisco to Boston by way of Cape Horn in a record-breaking 76 days, a record that*

CHALLENGE

by Pam Conrad

stood unchallenged for 140 years. And then, in 1993, a man from Boston set his mind, his heart, and all his sailing abilities on beating it.

A crowd of fans waves as *Great American II* ends its journey in Boston Harbor.

April 1993

After months of trial and error, more trials and worse luck, an exhausted but victorious Rich Wilson finally turned his trimaran, *Great American II*, due west toward home. He glanced up to the sails, checking to make sure they were set at the best angle to catch the wind. Finally Boston lay just ahead and Rich and his crewman Bill Biewenga were jubilant. They had been at sea for 69 days. It was April 7, 1993, and they were about to beat the phantom clipper ship home.

Rich felt the full impact of success when the Boston Harbor Light and Buoy came into view dead ahead. Weeks before, from a point off Recife, Brazil, he had radioed his mother: "For the first time we have Boston on

our bow. Keep the porch lights on, Mom, we're coming home." Now it was real, and ahead lay a hot shower, a floor that didn't continually heave and tip, and maybe a few friends and relatives to welcome them home.

His crewman Bill looked ahead and said, "I wonder if anyone will be there to meet us." Rich shrugged and together they watched the distant lighthouse grow closer and closer.

Meanwhile at the New England Aquarium in Boston Harbor, a school bus was unloading a class of fifth graders in the parking lot. They were all very excited and carried notebooks, a banner, and a few cameras. Also in the parking lot were camera crews and reporters from Boston television stations and newspapers. But they cleared a path for the students, because these were the special friends of Rich Wilson.

For over three months now these students and thousands like them from all over the United States and Canada, had followed the progress of *Great American II*, from the time it left San Francisco until this very day. Using their school computers with a special Prodigy program called Ocean Challenge, they learned about seamanship, geography, history, and much more.

The computer program had made it possible for the students to read Rich's daily log and even ask questions. "What do you miss the most?" they'd asked when the boat had been at sea for many weeks. Rich said he missed being able to stand up without holding onto something, and he missed friends, the news, and root beer floats. But he also knew that once he was on land, he would miss the fresh air of the sea. Rich had asthma and the stale polluted air in the city was a hardship for him. At sea, he breathed more easily.

"Why are you trying to break the record? What's the prize?" the students had asked. But there would be no prize for Rich, just the satisfaction of knowing he had tried three times, and had finally achieved his goal.

A crowd was gathering on the dock of the New England Aquarium where *Great American II* was expected to tie up. A reporter asked Rich's mother, "Where did your son get the idea for this race?" She told him how Rich had read a book about great sailing journeys by Carl Cutler called *Greyhounds of the Sea*. The book described the record-breaking journey of *Northern Light*. That's when Rich began to think about taking the challenge.

At the tiller of the homeward-bound trimaran, Rich Wilson had some

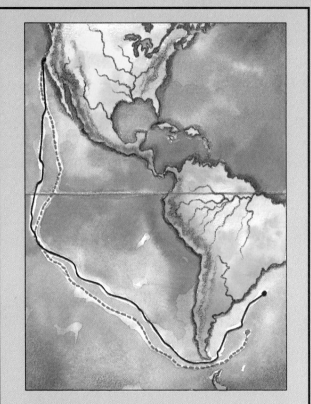

This map shows part of the route taken by *Great American II* from San Francisco to Boston. Rich and Bill navigated their trip by plotting their course on degrees of longitude. Longitude is a distance measured from an imaginary line, which runs from the North Pole through Greenwich, England, to the South Pole.

time to reflect. Soon he would tell reporters that "Many times a nagging uncertainty existed about whether it was worth it to pursue the dream this hard. Today, it became clear that it was." He had succeeded despite everything—despite his asthma, despite two failed attempts, despite wind and weather and the potential cruelty of the sea. King Neptune had finally smiled on him this last time.

October 1990

On his first attempt he had selected a 60-foot trimaran named *Great American.* It was a single-masted racing sailboat, built of fiberglass, and reinforced with Kevlar and carbon fiber, new boat-building materials. It had a central hull with a galley, a bunk, and a radio station. On each side of the main hull was a long pontoon, giving it, when at anchor, the look of a water-walking bug, and when in action, the awesome beauty of an eagle in flight.

Rich Wilson made his first attempt to beat *Northern Light*'s record with crewman Steve Pettengill, an experienced sailor who had already sailed *Great American.* They knew it was a good boat. It was

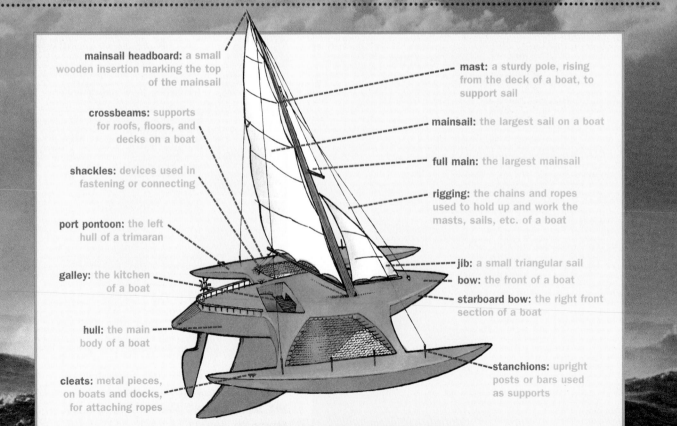

mainsail headboard: a small wooden insertion marking the top of the mainsail

crossbeams: supports for roofs, floors, and decks on a boat

shackles: devices used in fastening or connecting

port pontoon: the left hull of a trimaran

galley: the kitchen of a boat

hull: the main body of a boat

cleats: metal pieces, on boats and docks, for attaching ropes

mast: a sturdy pole, rising from the deck of a boat, to support sail

mainsail: the largest sail on a boat

full main: the largest mainsail

rigging: the chains and ropes used to hold up and work the masts, sails, etc. of a boat

jib: a small triangular sail

bow: the front of a boat

starboard bow: the right front section of a boat

stanchions: upright posts or bars used as supports

trimaran: *a boat with three hulls*

incredibly fast and virtually unsinkable. So they left San Francisco confidently on October 22, 1990, and sailed south along longitude 126 W, planning to sail around the Horn and then head north to Boston.

But the going was rough. The effort of skirting hurricanes and sailing into tempestuous winds took its toll on the boat. Rich and Steve had to repair crossbeams, replace shackles, and re-engineer the mainsail headboard.

Approaching Cape Horn a few days before Thanksgiving, *Great American* had a three-day lead on the phantom of *Northern Light*. Rich used sea maps called charts to keep a daily account of where *Northern Light* had been on her journey years before, and exactly where he was on his. *Great American* sailed its way through hailstorms and freezing winds that blew at 50 knots while the seas were building to 30-foot walls around them. Rich and Steve had to take down all its sails to prevent the boat from going too fast and somersaulting.

Then they tried throwing out five 100-foot lines over the stern or the back of the boat. (This has the same effect as dragging the soles of sneakers along the concrete to slow a speeding bicycle.) When this didn't work they added three more lines, tying them onto cleats and stanchions wherever they could, but the winds were increasing to 50 knots and the waves were building now to 40 feet. Soon they had to pull in all the lines and tie knots every ten feet in a desperate attempt to add enough drag to slow the boat and gain control.

All the time they were sailing Rich and Steve were getting reports and daily forecasts from a professional meteorologist, Bob Rice, and a shoreside router and interpreter, Bill Biewenga, who were in touch with them via radio from their offices in New England.

The following days grew worse and worse—howling winds screaming to 85 knots and foaming white seas rising to 60 feet and then crashing down all around them. There was no rest for Steve and Rich no matter how exhausted they felt. The seas around Cape Horn had a reputation for just this sort of madness and there was nowhere to turn for shelter.

On Thanksgiving Day, with no signs of conditions lessening, Rich and Steve were huddled below when suddenly the floor and walls of the cabin around them began to tilt. They braced themselves. *Great American* heeled farther and farther, too far, not righting herself. Then to their horror, she was heaved upside down.

It was smooth sailing for *Great American* when this picture was shot.

Standing on the ceiling of the cabin, shin deep in water, Rich and Steve grabbed their survival suits and struggled into them. With their radios now underwater, they had to turn on their "EPIRB"—an Emergency Position Indicator Radio Beacon. This beacon sent a distress message to a satellite in hopes that someone might pick up the signal on the radio. It also flashed a brilliant strobe, which was not at all helpful, as Rich and Bill had not seen another vessel for the last 300 miles. About an hour later, suddenly and unexpectedly, *Great American*'s cabin ceiling began to tilt beneath their feet. Again the boat heeled too far, only this time it was tossed into the air like a toy boat. When it hit the water, it was right-side up!

Rich and Steve were stunned. The mast and rigging were torn and in shambles, and draped into the water. All around them equipment lay destroyed. Every wave washed into the cabin and all about them debris floated—clothes, books, pots, a contact-lens case, and food.

Rich and Steve may have felt alone in the middle of a violent nightmare, but they were not. Far away in a New York Coast Guard Station, Lieutenant Brian Krenzien picked up their distress signal.

WHAT'S A SURVIVAL SUIT?

Faced with immersion in 41°F weather, Rich and Steve had a difficult decision to make. If they stayed in their wet suits, they risked hypothermia in the cold water. If they put on their survival suits, they would survive the cold, but they wouldn't be able to move around as easily. Together, they decided to use the survival suits. It was a decision that saved their lives! The catalogue entry to the right explains how a survival suit works.

COLD WATER SURVIVAL SUITS

SUIT SHOWN WITH OPTIONS

#340. STEARNS COLD WATER SURVIVAL SUIT
The Stearns survival suit provides the flotation & hypothermia protection you need to survive when forced into cold waters. Flotation is provided by the closed cell foam & inflatable flotation head pillow, so even if the suit is torn you still have total flotation. The material will also provide thermal protection - wet or dry! The hood, gloves & boots are sealed to the body of the suit to prevent the "flushing" of cold water into the suit. Donning time is less than 1 minute, even with persons totally unfamiliar with the suit. Tests done by the Hypothermia Water Safety Institute, Univ. of MN, showed the Stearns survival suit could provide survival time toward infinite in 35 degree water, a temperature where survival time is usually 30 minutes.

- GSA SIN #301-16, Expires 4-30-1994
- USCG approved Type V, complies with SOLAS 83.
- Less than 1 minute donning time.
- Unrestricted vision in excess of 120 degrees.
- Storage
- Impact tested; lightweight.
- Universally sized to avoid confusion in an emergency (weight range from 110-330 lbs., height range from 59" to 75")
- Five-finger gloves for improved dexterity.
- Color: Industrial Safety Orange.

He quickly scanned his computer for any ocean traffic that might be near them and found a container ship named *New Zealand Pacific* 100 miles away. He quickly got the ship through a satellite telephone link. "We have a distress signal. We would like you to divert to commence search." Captain David Watt responded immediately, turning his gigantic ship toward the position where *Great American* was supposed to be. He arrived nine hours later and sounded his horn, but in the howling wind Rich and Steve could not hear it. Luckily *New Zealand Pacific* spotted *Great American*'s strobe and the rescue began in earnest.

Meanwhile, Rich and Steve were huddled in a locker wondering how long they could stand the cold. Then Rich spotted lights in the distance, and out of the darkness came the huge ship, 815 feet long and weighing 41,000 tons. It came closer and closer. Its horn was blasting. It was clear that this mighty ship was coming to rescue them, but how would they ever get aboard it?

Soon the ship towered above them, rising and falling in the 65-foot waves. Then about 20 feet above sea level, a door opened in the ship's side, men appeared, light shone out, and a rope ladder and a net descended. The crew threw ropes across the awash trimaran.

Rich and Steve were wearing survival suits with awkward three-fingered gloves, but they quickly tied the ropes around their waists. Bracing themselves, Rich and Steve waited for just the right instant. Soon the water-logged trimaran rose in a swell and they made a dramatic leap, clung fiercely to the ladder and the net, and climbed up to the pilot door. They were saved!

Rich and Steve were tremendously relieved to be alive and warm. But the *New Zealand Pacific* was on its way to Holland and the racers would have to go along with them. Heartbroken, they tracked the lonely beam of *Great American* for some time, and then they lost sight of the boat in the sea forever.

A p r i l   1 9 9 3
Over two years later, that stormy night seemed so long ago. Rich wiped his eyes and eased the main a

bit. He was exhausted, but he was bringing her in.

Meanwhile back at the dock, more and more people were gathering. Everyone was excited and tense, hoping to be the first to catch a glimpse of the triumphant trimaran. Students hung the railings with banners reading *Welcome Home* and *Congratulations*.

The students who had followed *Great American II* on the computer line were especially excited. Every Monday, Wednesday, and Friday they had seen updated maps on their classroom computer screens that had shown exactly where Rich and Bill were. They had been able to read Rich's daily log. And they were able to ask questions of the sailors as well, questions that went instantly from their classroom to *Great American II*'s home

office in Boston and then by satellite telex to Rich's laptop computer on board.

"Is there anything you forgot or wish you brought along with you on your trip? Sincerely Lauren"

"How many whales have you seen? from Scott"

"Do you worry about hurricanes? from Arin"

One student asked, "What is the first thing you will do if you beat *Northern Light*'s record?"

Rich answered, "Whether we break the record or not, I'll go to the bow of *Great American II*, pat her and thank her for defending us as we guided her, give my mom a big hug, and go into the Italian section of Boston for a big spaghetti dinner with my friends!"

The students on the dock kept their eyes riveted to the water. Soon all they had learned and read on their computers would be turning to real life before their eyes. They would see *Great American II* for themselves and actually meet the crew!

January 1993

After losing the original *Great American* in 1990, Rich had worked hard for two years to get additional support and sponsoring to find a new boat. Finally

he purchased another trimaran, just like his first, only seven feet shorter. It was named *Great American II* and Rich and Bill Biewenga, his new crewman, were given a rousing send-off by family and friends as they headed out once more.

Less than a day out they ran into a storm with 55-knot winds. They changed the sails six times, from a full main, down to the smallest mainsail with no jib. The sea was rising 15 to 25 feet around them. Then a wave smashed into them, and when the water receded, the bow of their port pontoon was gone.

Barely begun, they had to turn back to San Francisco for repairs. There, an incredible marvel of cooperation and teamwork came together. From all across the country, friends who heard about *Great American II*'s dilemma and believed in the project rushed to help.

more, stronger and more determined than ever. And it was this third try, followed step-by-step by students around the country, that finally had King Neptune's blessing.

Life on board was a challenge. Rich and Bill took turns navigating and sleeping in two- or three-hour shifts. Sometimes Rich would be ready to turn in when a new weather map would start to print out and his curiosity would get the better of him.

Crewman Bill found it especially hard to sleep while the ocean was tossing the boat around. He even resorted to tying a pillow to his head so that his head wouldn't bounce like a coconut off the cabin ceiling.

But both men enjoyed the sights of nature that were all around them, and reported regularly their sightings of dolphins, whales, albatross, flying fish, and once, in the sky, a full double rainbow.

As time passed and they drew closer to the southern tip of South America, the weather turned colder and colder. They each had to wear

There was Peter Hogg, who held the solo San Francisco-to-Tokyo record; Walter Greene, a multi-hull designer, builder and racer from Maine; Bud Sutherland, a veteran ocean racer and boatyard manager from South Carolina; Ed Sisk, a solo trans-atlantic racer from Connecticut; and Marc Ginisty, a talented multi-hull builder. Together they created an incredible team. Working around the clock in the rain, they rebuilt the missing port bow and reinforced the starboard bow in ten days. Then Rich asked his Prodigy users if he should count these lost days as race time, or if he should start the clock again.

Everyone agreed that the clock would begin again. So on January 27th, Rich and Bill headed out once

Rich and Bill work together to sail *Great American II.*

two layers of socks, sea boots, a jacket, foul weather gear, a stocking cap, a safety harness, and at night, a headlight like miners wear. One night in total exhaustion, Rich fell asleep at the tiller and woke when he collapsed onto the cockpit floor.

As each day passed, Rich's last near-fatal encounter with Cape Horn was never far from his mind. But this time, his luck was good. The weather held, and through a mist Rich and Bill were able to watch the Horn's light flashing every five seconds. The Cape's foreboding rocks and inhospitable cliffs held the sailors spellbound. Here many had died fighting the storms and waves. But at last, as *Northern Light* had done years before, *Great American II* sailed on past.

They were not home free, though. The worst was surely behind them, but there were still another 7,000 miles to go, and they were not easy miles. Rich and Bill were exhausted, and when the sea was rough a couple of days from Bermuda, they were not sure they would make it. They had to cross the tumultuous Gulf Stream, and at the southern edge of George's Bank, where it was shallow and windy, they

experienced the most bitter cold they had known.

A p r i l   1 9 9 3
But now at last, it was all behind them. Jubilantly, Rich and Bill sailed across the line *Northern Light* had crossed years before, and the pop of a final gun announced their victory.

Ahead they saw a small flotilla of welcoming vessels, and cannon shots rang in the air. As tired as they were, Rich and Bill were suddenly full of energy. Ahead of them a Boston fireboat spouted a majestic torrent of water in the air and led them in.

"There!" someone shouted. "There! I see them!" Hundreds of onlookers now lined the docks. Fingers pointed, hands clapped and all eyes turned to the harbor where

Great American II nears the finish line.

boats were coming in. There the crowd caught its first glimpse of a tall mast pointing up into the sky, and soon all of *Great American II* came into sight with its pontoons spread proudly on both sides. Its mainsail was up and with a soft and gentle wind, Rich turned it toward the dock.

Rich shaded his eyes and tried to see exactly where he had to take *Great American II* to tie it up. For weeks now he hadn't been near land or docks, and he felt a little uncertain handling the boat in such tight quarters.

"Look at all those people," Rich said, pointing. "I wonder what's going on at the aquarium today."

Slowly they approached the dock and that's when they realized why everyone was there. A large computer banner read "Welcome Home, Rich and Bill!"

Bill and Rich are welcomed home.

Bill grinned and then started to laugh. "I think *we're* happening at the aquarium today."

Rich and Bill stared in amazement. Slowly they began to pick out familiar faces in the cheering crowd—faces of the people who had helped with communications from the home office, faces of some of the people who had helped rebuild *Great American II* in San Francisco, faces of friends, supporters, family members, and then the faces of the children. Rich and Bill realized how many children were there. The dock was teeming with kids and they were all smiling and cheering and waving their heroes home.

Ocean Challenge
A NEWSPAPER IN EDUCATION PROGRAM

SOURCE

Prodigy
Computer
Network

TEAMWORK

by Rich Wilson

To be on a team one must accept the team's goals—not just intellectually, but emotionally and viscerally. For when the going gets rough, the heart will dig in where the mind may rationalize.

Aboard *Great American II*, Bill and I are in a unique situation. Being only two, we have placed our lives in each other's hands. Though starkly dramatic here, the concept is transferable onshore, where many teams depend on every teammate.

A team's chemistry is evolutionary. Aboard *GA II*, we are coworkers and roommates, working 168-hour weeks for 11 weeks. That activity and intensity are difficult, so we must consciously work at the team dynamic. We must know when to check our egos, when to vent frustrations, when to pick the other up, when to absorb extra sacrifice.

Yet every team needs a leader (at sea, the skipper) and a chain of command. The leader must balance authority with the need to keep information flowing up as well as down, both to make for better decisions and so that team

SHIP'S LOG

3/11/93 Day 43
- 5 days ahead of N.L.
- 9,156 nautical miles sailed
- Barograph at 1019mb
- 10 knots of wind from west
- No rain this week
- Air temperature: 70°F
- Calm seas

members know that they have input. At sea, Bill and I decide sail changes and strategic weather routing constantly. When on watch, he sails the boat his way, with the proviso that major changes/decisions must fall in the skipper's lap.

Our team can also be viewed more broadly. Ocean Challenge is not just Bill and me at sea, but is Trip Lowell and Lyon Osborn in our Boston office, the NIE staffs at 12 major newspapers, their 10,000 teachers and 250,000 students, Prodigy and their members, our two imaginative regional sponsors, the American Lung Association, our Board of Directors and 14 visionary shareholders, our equipment sponsors, our ham radio contacts, etc.

Though the more visible tip of the iceberg, Bill and I know and are glad that we have these teammates.

Sea-Fever

I must go down to the seas again, to the lonely sea and the sky,

And all I ask is a tall ship and a star to steer her by;

And the wheel's kick and the wind's song and the white sail's shaking,

And the gray mist on the sea's face, and a gray dawn breaking.

I must go down to the seas again, for the call of the running tide

Is a wild call and a clear call that may not be denied;

And all I ask is a windy day with the white clouds flying,

And the flung spray and the blown spume, and the seagulls crying.

I must go down to the seas again, to the vagrant gypsy life,

To the gull's way and the whale's way where the wind's like a whetted knife;

And all I ask is a merry yarn from a laughing fellow-rover,

And quiet sleep and a sweet dream when the long trick's over.

by John Masefield
illustrated by Raul Colon

How to
Publish a Travel Magazine

Build a publishing *team* and create a *magazine* that will entice others to travel.

Visitors to a travel agency will find plenty of travel magazines to browse through. Travel magazines provide pictures and articles about vacation spots around the world. Travelers might read travel magazines for ideas about where to travel or for information about destinations they've already chosen. It takes a team of writers, artists, and researchers to publish a really exciting travel magazine.

TERRIFIC TRAVEL

In this issue:

Top Ten Dream Vacations

Page 10

1 Choose a Focus

What would you like to read about in a travel magazine? With your team, decide on a focus for your magazine. Perhaps each teammate could write an article about his or her dream vacation. Or you might focus on one destination, with each teammate exploring something different about it. You could devote your magazine to budget travel, or to a comparison of great theme parks. For more ideas, browse through some travel magazines and think about what makes them particularly appealing or useful. Think also about what sort of audience you'd like your magazine to target.

TOOLS

- paper and pencil
- research materials
- art supplies
- photos

Tip If you completed Workshop 2, you might want to publish a travel magazine article about the destination you chose for your itinerary.

2. Plan Your Magazine

Make a list of all the articles and features you'd like to include in your magazine—first-person travel narratives; interviews with well-traveled friends; well-researched articles about dream destinations; charts, graphs, and maps; and so on. Decide how each teammate will contribute. Some of you might research and write articles while others locate photographs or create illustrations to accompany the articles. One or two teammates might take charge of laying out the finished contributions and making a cover and a table of contents. If you find yourself with more jobs than teammates, decide as a group which features to drop. Make a list of each teammate's assignment to use as a checklist when it's time to publish the magazine. Review the list to make sure you haven't neglected any important jobs.

How Am I Doing?

Before your team begins to put your magazine together, take a minute to ask yourself these questions:

- Has the team decided on a focus for the magazine?

- Have all the articles, columns, and features been assigned?

- Does everyone on the team have an assignment?

Complete your magazine assignment. If you are writing an article or looking for photos, you might have to go to the library to do some research. Here are a few more suggestions.

Writers: Ask your teammates for ideas. Look at their travel brochures and itineraries for information.

Illustrators/Photo Researchers: If you're looking for photos or drawing illustrations for a specific article, make sure you know what it's about! Postcards might make good illustrations. See if you have any at home, and ask your teammates to bring some, too.

Cover artists: Try to think up a cover design or illustration that will tie together everything inside the magazine. Explain your ideas to your teammates and get their feedback.

Everyone: Make sure your completed assignments are neat, clean, and ready to be published!

4 Publish Your Magazine

When all of your magazine copy is complete and the illustrations are ready, it's time to publish your travel magazine. Those team members who are in charge of layout should collect all of the articles and illustrations, and work together to come up with a creative and appealing layout for the magazine. When they are ready to put everything together, they might call a meeting of the whole team, to get their teammates' final input before publishing the magazine.

When all of the teams in your class have published their magazines, hold a Travel Day. Present your magazine in class, and exchange magazines with the other teams. Discover new places you'd like to explore!

If You Are Using a Computer ...

Create your travel magazine on the computer, using the Newsletter format. Browse through clip art to find maps for your magazine.

CONGRATULATIONS

You've found out how teammates can work together to plan a successful voyage or explore a new destination.

Marie French
Travel Agent ▶

Glossary

adze (adz) *noun*
A tool with a sharp, curved blade for trimming and shaping wood.

bro•chures
(brō shŏŏrs′) *noun*
Informational pamphlets or booklets. ▲ **brochure**

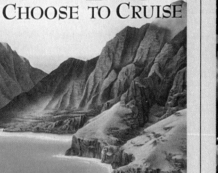
travel brochure

ca•ca•o (kə kä′ō) *noun*
A tropical tree. Its seeds, or beans, are the source of cocoa and chocolate.

Fact File

The people of Central America and Mexico once used cacao beans as money.

cacao beans

car•i•bou
(kar′ə bōō) *noun*
A large deer, related to the reindeer.

Fact File

The female caribou is the only American female deer, besides the reindeer, that has antlers.

caribou

caulked (kôkt) *verb*
Made seams watertight or airtight by applying a sealing substance. ▲ **caulk**

cli•ents (klī´ ənts) *noun*
Customers; people who use the service of another person or organization. The lawyer scored a big victory for her *clients*.
▲ **client**

cross•wind
(krôs´wind´) *noun*
A wind that blows across the path of an object.

des•ti•na•tion
(des´ tə nā´sh´ ən) *noun*
The place to which a person is traveling.

ex•pe•di•tion
(ek´spi dish´ ən) *noun*
A trip, taken by a group of people, to explore a region for a specific purpose.

fau•na (fô´nə) *noun*
All of the animals commonly found in a certain region.

flight plan
(flīt´ plan´) *noun*
A report describing the route of an upcoming flight. A *flight plan* is given to an air traffic control facility, either orally or in writing.

Word History

Flora is related to the Spanish word **flor**, meaning "flower."

---

flo•ra (flôr ə´) *noun*
All of the plants commonly found in a certain region.

foul weath•er gear
(foul´ weth´ər gēr) *noun*
Special clothing and tools used for protection against extreme bad weather.

fre•quen•cy
(frē´ kwən sē) *noun*
The particular number of cycles per second at which a radio station can be tuned in or contacted. If one *frequency* is blocked, try tuning into another.

hang•ar (hang´ər) *noun*
A shed, or shelter, in which airplanes are stored and repaired.

hangar

hull (hul) *noun*
The body of a ship.

in•ac•ces•si•ble
(in´ək ses´ə bəl)
adjective
Impossible to reach or contact.

a	add	o͝o	took	ə =
ā	ace	o͞o	pool	a in *above*
â	care	u	up	e in *sicken*
ä	palm	û	burn	i in *possible*
e	end	y͞oo	fuse	o in *melon*
ē	equal	oi	oil	u in *circus*
i	it	ou	pout	
ī	ice	ng	ring	
o	odd	th	thin	
ō	open	th	this	
ô	order	zh	vision	

Glossary

i·tin·er·ar·y
(i tin′ə rer′ ē) *noun*
A plan or a record of
a journey.

keel (kēl) *noun*
A central piece that runs the
length of a ship's bottom
and plays an important role
in holding together the ship.

li·a·nas (lē än′əs) *noun*
Woody vines common in
tropical forests. ▲ liana

liana

lines (līnz) *noun*
Ropes or cables attached to
a boat. Throw me the *lines*
so that I can tie up the
boat. ▲ line

log (lôg) *noun*
A book containing the
official daily records of a
ship's voyage. Christopher
Columbus kept a detailed
log, of his journeys to the
New World.

maiden voy·age
(mād′n voi′ij) *noun*
A person's or a vehicle's
first journey.

ma·lar·i·a
(mə lâr′ē ə) *noun*
A disease that is caused
by the bite of certain
mosquitoes. It is usually
accompanied by high
fever, chills, and sweats.

mar·ten (mär′tən) *noun*
A small animal, similar to a
weasel, with a slender body,
soft fur, and a bushy tail.

Fact File

The marten is a common
animal in northern North
America.

marten

nav·i·gat·ing
(nav′i gat ing) *verb*
Controlling the course of
something (usually a ship,
boat, or plane).

Word History

Navigate is based on a
Latin word, **navis**, which
means "ship."

pro•pel•ler
(prə pel′ər) *noun*
The revolving shaft, with blades, that moves a ship or plane forward.

propeller

ruffs (rufs) *noun*
Rings of feathers or fur extending outward, usually around the neck. ▲ **ruff**

ruff

ship•wright
(ship′rīt′) *noun*
A person who builds or does carpentry work on ships.

sites (sīts) *noun*
Places where buildings or cities are located. ▲ **site**

sub-ze•ro
(sub zēr′ō) *adjective*
Below zero. After weeks of *sub-zero* temperatures, the lakes were frozen solid.

till•er (til′ər) *noun*
The handle of a boat's rudder; the helm.

trans•con•ti•nen•tal
(trans′kon tn en′tl)
adjective
Extending from one side of a continent to the other.

Fact File

Amelia Earhart was the first woman to complete a solo transcontinental flight in the United States.

trap•line
(trap′lin) *noun*
An area where traps are set.

trib•u•tar•ies
(trib′yə ter´ēz) *noun*
Streams or rivers that flow into larger streams or rivers. ▲ **tributary**

wing•tip
(wing′tip) *noun*
The outer end of an airplane wing.

a	add	o͝o	took	ə =	
ā	ace	o͞o	pool	a in *above*	
â	care	u	up	e in *sicken*	
ä	palm	û	burn	i in *possible*	
e	end	yo͞o	fuse	o in *melon*	
ē	equal	oi	oil	u in *circus*	
i	it	ou	pout		
ī	ice	ng	ring		
o	odd	th	thin		
ō	open	th	this		
ô	order	zh	vision		

Authors & Illustrators

Betsy Byars *pages 10–23*

The event that inspired *Coast to Coast* was a trip that Betsy Byars herself took. A few years ago, she learned how to pilot a plane, and she and her husband made a cross-country trek in a Piper Cub. Byars has written many books for children and has won numerous awards, including the Newbery Medal.

"My books usually begin with something that really happened, a newspaper story or an event in my children's lives."

Pam Conrad *pages 114–126*

When she's not busy writing, you can find this author sailing the open seas. She owns her own sailboat and enjoys sailing off the coast of Long Island, New York, where she makes her home. Although most of her books are fiction, Pam Conrad says a little bit of her life is in everything she writes.

Kirkpatrick Hill *pages 52–67*

This author is no stranger to the Alaskan wilderness she writes about. She grew up in Alaska, and returned there later to become a teacher in the Alaskan bush. "Life in the Alaskan bush is very adventurous, and strange things are always happening," Hill says.

Peter Lourie *pages 72–87*

With a background as colorful as the places he explores, Peter Lourie is a natural travel writer. He has worked in some of the world's greatest museums, located in Africa, London, and New York City. In 1991, he began using his writing skills to share his travels with young readers. Besides the Amazon River, Lourie has written about the Hudson and Yukon Rivers in the United States.

David Macaulay *pages 94–113*

Before he began writing books, this award-winning author and illustrator earned a degree in architecture. Now David Macaulay uses words and pictures to take his readers on fascinating architectural tours of places such as medieval castles and the Egyptian pyramids. His knowledge of design has also helped him to write and illustrate books such as *Ship* and *The Way Things Work*. Macaulay continues to create books in his Rhode Island studio.

"One of the things I try to do in a picture is to make the reader more of a participant than a spectator."

John Masefield *pages 128–129*

Born in 1878 in England, John Masefield sailed on a merchant ship when he was just fourteen years old. He gave up his life at sea a few years later, after meeting some of England's most famous poets. Masefield then moved to London, where he became the editor of a literary magazine. Eventually, he became a well-known poet himself. Masefield died in 1967.

Author/Illustrator Study

More by David Macaulay

City
Ancient Rome comes to life in this book about the building of the city.

Pyramid
Wonderfully detailed pictures reveal the process involved in building these amazing structures of ancient Egypt.

The Way Things Work
This incredible book describes how many important inventions work. *The Way Things Work* is also available on CD-ROM.

Fiction

The Borrowers Aloft
by Mary Norton
The adventures of the tiny Clock family continue as the Borrowers build a balloon and make a daring escape from greedy kidnappers.

Pedro's Journal
by Pam Conrad
This historical novel is written from the point of view of a cabin boy who sailed with Christopher Columbus.

Tough Boy and Sister
by Kirkpatrick Hill
In this suspenseful adventure, the children from *Winter Camp* find themselves stranded for the summer at a camp down a remote branch of the Yukon River.

Nonfiction

Around the World in a Hundred Years
by Jean Fritz
The European explorers of the 1600s traveled far and wide. The information they brought home helped make for more accurate world maps.

Lost Star
by Patricia Lauber
Amelia Earhart was one of the most famous and beloved aviators of her day. Her exciting life and her mysterious disappearance are detailed in this biography.

Space Challenger: The Story of Guion Bluford
by James Haskins and Kathleen Benson
Guion Bluford was the first African-American astronaut. This story of his life includes many details about how he trained for his career.

xMedia

 **Videos**

African Journey
Public Media

Luke, a self-centered Canadian teenager, travels with his father to Africa, where he meets Themba. As Luke and his new friend travel together, Luke discovers more about himself. (3 hours)

Homeward Bound: The Incredible Journey
Disney

Three loyal pets—two dogs and a cat—face one obstacle after another as they journey across Canada to find their way home. (90 minutes)

Where in the World: Kids Explore Mexico
Encounter Video

This Emmy Award-winning title is one in a series of tapes that explores geography, history, and culture. Here, a group of middle schoolers receives a letter from a Mexican pen pal, which inspires them to learn more about Mexico. (40 minutes)

Software

Swamp Gas
Inline Design
(IBM, MAC)

Plan an itinerary and visit a variety of interesting places as you help the lovable space creature, Swamp Gas, explore American geography.

Wayzata World Factbook
(IBM, MAC)

This factbook contains travel advisories from around the world, as well as maps, photos, charts, and graphs.

Language Discovery
Applied Optical Media
(IBM, MAC, CD-ROM)

If you want to travel, it helps to know other languages. This program can help you learn 1,000 words in English, French, German, and Spanish.

Magazines

Odyssey
Cobblestone Publishing

The articles in *Odyssey* are all about space travel and exploration.

Dolphin Log
Cousteau Society

The log offers great photos and lots of information about the sea. Learn how teams of divers, sailors, and scientists work together to find out more about aquatic creatures.

National Geographic World
National Geographic Society

World is filled with stories of exciting international adventures, profiles of children in faraway places, and letters from students all over the world.

A Place to Write

**Cousteau Society
930 W. 21st Street
Norfolk, VA 23517**

Write here to find out more about unusual life in the deep.

Acknowledgments

Grateful acknowledgment is made to the following sources for permission to reprint from previously published material. The publisher has made diligent efforts to trace the ownership of all copyrighted material in this volume and believes that all necessary permissions have been secured. If any errors or omissions have inadvertently been made, proper corrections will gladly be made in future editions.

Cover: © Augustus Butera for Scholastic Inc.

Interior: Selection and cover from COAST TO COAST by Betsy Byars. Copyright © 1992 by Betsy Byars. Used by permission of Delacorte Press, a division of Bantam Doubleday Dell Publishing Group, Inc.

"Country Rolls Out Tarmac for Girl Pilot" and "City Girl Is High-Flying Pilot" from *The Meadville Tribune*, 9/21/93 and 5/26/93. Reprinted by permission. Selection from Vicki Van Meter/Bryant Gumbel interview transcript and logo copyright © National Broadcasting Company, Inc. All rights reserved. Courtesy of the *TODAY* Show.

Selection and cover from GOING PLACES: THE YOUNG TRAVELER'S GUIDE AND ACTIVITY BOOK by Harriet Webster. Text copyright © 1991 by Harriet Webster. Jacket illustration copyright © 1991 by Gail Owens. Reprinted by arrangement with Atheneum Books for Young Readers, Simon and Schuster Children's Publishing Division. Amtrak's Sunset Limited Time Table used by permission of the National Railroad Passenger Corporation.

Selection and cover from SURVIVE IN FIVE LANGUAGES by Ceris Farnes, illustrated by Ann Johns. Copyright © 1992 by Usborne Publishing Ltd. Published in the U.K. by Usborne Publishing Ltd. and in the U.S. by EDC Publishing, Tulsa, OK. Reprinted with permission.

Brochure on Cheekwood, Tennessee Botanical Gardens and Museum of Art. By permission of Cheekwood, Nashville, TN 37205. Brochure on Ryman Auditorium. Used by permission of Ryman Auditorium, Nashville, TN 37219. Brochure on The Parthenon, Nashville, TN. Used by permission of the Metropolitan Board of Parks and Recreation, Nashville, TN 37201.

Selection and cover from WINTER CAMP by Kirkpatrick Hill. Copyright © 1993 by Kirkpatrick Hill. Reprinted by arrangement with Margaret K. McElderry Books, Simon & Schuster Children's Publishing Division. Cover used by permission of the artist, John Little.

"Trail of Courage" and logo from *Action* Magazine, October 6, 1989. Copyright © 1989 by Scholastic Inc. Reprinted by permission.

"The Road and the Fire," "Indians," and cover from AMAZON by Peter Lourie with photographs by Marcos Santilli. Text copyright © 1991 by Peter Lourie. Photographs copyright © 1991 by Marcos Santilli. Published by Caroline House, an imprint of Boyds Mills Press, Inc. Reprinted by permission.

"Washington, D.C. Getaway" from Domenico Tours USA & CANADA ESCORTED TOURS booklet, 1995. Used by permission of Domenico Tours, Bayonne, NJ 07002.

Selection and cover from SHIP by David Macaulay. Copyright © 1993 by David Macaulay. Reprinted by permission of Houghton Mifflin Co. All rights reserved.

"Teamwork" by Rich Wilson is from *Ocean Challenge Newspaper*, which appeared on Prodigy. Used by permission of Rich Wilson who owns all rights.

"Sea Fever" from POEMS by John Masefield (New York: Macmillan, 1953). Used by permission of the Society of Authors as the literary representative of the estate of John Masefield.

Cover from DESTINATION: ANTARCTICA by Robert Swan. Photograph copyright © 1988 by Robert Swan. Published by Scholastic Inc.

Cover from FLYING FREE: AMERICA'S FIRST BLACK AVIATORS by Philip S. Hart. Photographs courtesy of Smithsonian Institution (top and bottom right), Philip S. Hart (bottom left). Published by Lerner Publications Company.

Cover from THE ILLYRIAN ADVENTURE by Lloyd Alexander, illustrated by Michael Conway. Illustration copyright © 1990 by Dell Publishing. Published by Dell Publishing, a division of Bantam Doubleday Dell Publishing Group, Inc.

Cover from MR. POPPER'S PENGUINS by Richard and Florence Atwater, illustrated by Robert Lawson. Copyright © 1938 by Richard and Florence Atwater, renewed 1966 by Florence Atwater, Doris Atwater, and Carroll Atwater Bishop. Published by Little Brown & Company, Inc.

Photography and Illustration Credits

Photos: © John Lei for Scholastic Inc., all Tool Box items unless otherwise noted. pp. 2-3: © Steve Leonard for Scholastic Inc. except for p. 3 tc: © Rhoda Sidney/Photo Edit. p. 4 c: © Ana Esperanza Nance for Scholastic Inc.; tc: © Rhoda Sidney/PhotoEdit. p. 5 c: © Ana Esperanza Nance for Scholastic Inc.; tc: © Rhoda Sidney/PhotoEdit. p. 6 c: © Michael Newman/PhotoEdit; tc: © Rhoda Sidney/PhotoEdit. pp. 8-9 c: © Russ Kinne/Comstock, Inc. p. 24 c: © Pat Wellenback/AP Wide World Photos. pp. 24-25 background: © Michael P. Gadomski/FPG International Corp. p. 25 c: © Robert F. Bukaty/AP Wide World Photos. p. 26 tc: © Rick Bowmer/AP Wide World Photos; bc: © J. Pat/Gamma Liaison International. pp. 26-27 background: © Jeffrey Sylvester/FPG International Corp. p. 27 br: © Chris Kasson/AP Wide World Photos; tl: © Christopher Horner/Meadville Tribune/AP Wide World Photos. p. 28 tl: Courtesy of NBC. pp. 28-29 background: © Halley Ganges for Scholastic Inc. p. 29 bc: Courtesy of NBC. pp. 32-33: Halley Ganges for Scholastic Inc. p. 35 tr, bc: © Stephanie Bart-Horvarth; tl; br: © Ana Esperanza Nance for Scholastic Inc. p. 36 tr: © Comstock, Inc.; bc: Images from left to right: © Peter Gridley/FPG International Corp.; © Telegraph Colour Library/FPG International Corp.; © Tony Stone Images, Inc.; © Churchill & Mehr/Tony Stone Images, Inc.; © Peter Gridley/FPG International Corp.; © George Chan/Photo Researchers, Inc. p. 38 bl: © Bie Bostrom for Scholastic Inc. p. 42 tc: Rhoda Sidney/Photo Edit. p. 43 cr; br: © John Bessler for Scholastic Inc. pp. 42-45: © Steve Leonard for Scholastic Inc. p. 46 bl: © Jeff Divine/FPG International Corp.; tr: Tennessee Botanical Gardens and Museum of Art. pp.46-47 background: © Kathleen Hanzel/Tony Stone Images, Inc. p. 47 bl: Ryman Auditorium, Nashville, TN; tc: © The Parthenon, Nashville, TN/Metropolitan Board of Parks and Recreation; br: © David Stoecklin/The Stock Market. pp. 48-49 bc: Stanley Bach for Scholastic Inc. p. 49 br: © Steve Leonard for Scholastic Inc. pp. 50-51 c: © Terry & Group Mackay Id/The Stock Market. pp. 68-69 c: Courtesy of Amway Corp. p. 70 tl: Courtesy of Amway Corp.; all others: © Beedell/Sipa Press. p. 71: Beedell/Sipa Press. p. 72 map of Amazon: © ARPA. p. 88 bl: © Ed Wheeler/The Stock Market; br: © Wes Thompson/The Stock Market. p. 90 bc: © Stanley Bach for Scholastic Inc. p. 91 br: © Steve Leonard for Scholastic Inc. pp. 92-93 © Nicolas LeCorre/Gamma Liaison International. pp. 114-115 © Telegraph Colour Library/FPG International Corp. p. 115 c: © Ocean Challenge. p. 116 tc: © Telegraph Colour Library/FPG International Corp.; tr: © Daniel Forster/Stock Newport. pp. 118-119 background: © Tony Stone Images, INc. p. 119 tr: © Bill Biewenga/Stock Newport. p. 120 bc: © Ocean Challenge; bl: © Telegraph Colour Library/FPG International Corp. p. 121 tc: © Courtesy of Stearns Manufacturing. p. 122 tl, br: © Telegraph Colour Library/FPG International Corp.; inset © Bill Biewenga/Stock Newport. p. 123 tc: © Daniel Forster/Stock Newport; tr: © Telegraph Colour Library/FPG International Corp. pp. 124-125 background: © Warren Bolster/Tony Stone Images, Inc.; p. 124 tl: © Bill Biewenga/Stock Newport. p. 125 tr: © Bill Biewenga/Stock Newport; c, br: © Daniel Forster/Stock Newport. p. 126 inset: © Daniel Forster/Stock Newport; tl, br: © Telegraph Colour Library/FPG International Corp. p. 130: © Don Sparks/The Image Bank. p. 131 background: © Bruce Coleman Inc.; c: © Stanley Bach for Scholastic Inc. p. 132 bl: © Chad Slattery/Tony Stone Images, Inc.; br: © Fredrick McKinney/FPG International Corp. p. 133 bl: © Michael Hart/FPG International Corp.; cr: © Stanley Bach for Scholastic Inc. p. 134: © Stanley Bach for Scholastic Inc. p. 135 bl: © Stanley Bach for Scholastic Inc.; br: © Steve Leonard for Scholastic Inc. p. 136 cr: © Jim Zipp/Photo Researchers, Inc.; c: © Toma D.W. Friedman/Photo Researchers, Inc.; bl: © Steve Leonard for Scholastic Inc. p. 137 cr: © Will & Deni McIntyre/Photo Researchers, Inc. p. 138 cr: © Pat & Tom Leeson/Photo Researchers, Inc.; bc: © Tom McHugh/Photo Researchers, Inc. p. 139 tc: © Tom McHugh/Photo Researchers, Inc.; cl: © Russ Kinne/Comstock, Inc. p. 140 tl: © Courtesy of Scholastic Trade Department; cl: © Sarah Conrad. p. 141 tr: © Courtesy Boyds Mills Press; cr: © Houghton Mifflin, David Macauley; p 141 br: UPI/Beltmann Newsphotos. p. 142 cl: © David Sutherland/Tony Stone Images Inc. c: © The Granger Collection. p. 143 br: © Stanley Bach for Scholastic Inc.

Illustrations: pp. 30-34, 36, 38-39: Santiago Cohen; p. 40: Susan Pizzo; pp. 52-62, 64-67: Shonto Begay; pp. 128-129: Raul Colon.

144